LION & LAMB

A Preaching Series based on the life of the Shepherd King

C. MICHAEL MILLS

C.S.S. Publishing Co., Inc.

Lima, Ohio

DAVID, LION AND LAMB

Copyright © 1988 by
The C.S.S. Publishing Company, Inc.
Lima, Ohio

Library of Congress Cataloging-in-Publication Data

Mills, Michael. 1947-
    David, lion and lamb / Michael Mills.
        p.   cm.
    ISBN 1-556-73029-2
    1. Bible. O.T. Samuel — Sermons.   2. David, King of Israel — Sermons. 3. Presbyterian Church — Sermons. 4. Sermons. American. I.Title.
BS1325.4.M55 1988
222'.40924—dc19   87-30933
                                                                    CIP

8814 / ISBN 1-55673-029-2   PRINTED IN U.S.A.

"In the end he formed a true picture

of the gallant and gentle-hearted man,

a mingling of a lion and lamb . . ."[1]

[1]Victor Hugo, *Les Miserables*, Penguin Classics Edition, Penguin-Viking, Inc., Harmondsworth, England, 1982, p. 541.

Table of Contents

Introduction

Welcome to the pages of *David, Lion and Lamb*. In the few hours it takes to read this book you will meet one of the most fascinating persons in the Old Testament. David's name in Hebrew means "Beloved of God." Throughout his stormy life of roller coaster highs and lows, he was loved by a God of the valleys and the precipices. As I have researched the life and faith of David, I have opened up previously unexplored vistas of my own heart. In David I have met myself. In him I have seen how a man may suffer depression, defeat, and doubt, and conquer them through a granite-like faith in God.

David was a Renaissance man centuries before Michelangelo was commissioned to sculpt the shepherd king for a wealthy Florentine merchant-prince. David was a *warrior* of daring strategic genius who would have been comfortable discussing strategy with Napoleon or Stonewall Jackson. The bard of Bethlehem was a poet and songwriting genius whose words mirror the gamut of human emotion from deep depression to ecstatic joy. The Psalter of David is a glimpse into the soul, not only of a great *poet*, but of a great pilgrim people. To read the psalms is to pluck on the harpstrings of the human heart. David was a *ruler* of vision as he united his people around the Ark of the Covenant, which he wisely moved to centrally located Jerusalem. David was a troubled *husband* and *father* whose domestic crises speak to our own age of familial conflict.

Primarily, though, David was a sinful human. The Bible portrays him, warts and all. His infatuous love affair with Bathsheba is told with candor. But his humble repentance before God, and his forgiveness for national and personal wrongdoing resonate in American minds, as we recall such relatively recent affairs as Watergate and other corruption in high places.

David is a man of God. A person worth knowing. Whether he is an old friend first met in a Sunday church school classroom or in a story your parents told you while young, or you have never studied him before, I hope you will be enriched by this book.

Pastors may find the book useful as they prepare a sermon or lecture series on the life of David and his times based upon the Common Lectionary readings (Cycle B) for the Old Testament.

Bible college and seminary students may find the book useful in homiletic courses in which their task is to translate Old Testament age material into messages which will speak to parishioners living in the nuclear age world we call home.

Church officers may find the book useful in a study dealing with the temptations and triumphs possible to those placed in leadership roles in church and synagogue.

Shepherds of the lonely, sick, and aged may use the book as a gift for someone needing encouragement in the hospital/nursing home/sick room environment. It is hoped that the work will strengthen faith and rekindle enthusiasm for service to the God of David and each of us.

Thank yous are due my wife Dalinda for her typing of the manuscript, and for her words of encouragement and support. My parents, Charlie and Bettye Mills are also thanked, for a lifetime of love and wisdom. They have been my good shepherds, as they taught me to worship the Great Shepherd of the Sheep, Jesus Christ. My editor at C.S.S. Publishing Company, Dawn Lausa, has proved helpful with her editorial assistance. As with my earlier book, *Dirty Hands, Pure Hearts*, Michael Sherer, chief editor at C.S.S., has been encouraging in his support.

This book is dedicated to everyone committed to "faith in search of understanding."

The Eighth Son

1 Samuel 16:1-13
Proper 4 (May 29-June 4)

"Play it again, Sam." A legendary song request made by Humphrey Bogart in a Casablanca bar. A lamentation chanted by the daughters of Israel. A retreating cry of a battered and beaten army. A tear-stained cry wrung from the throats of mothers and fathers grieving over slain sons. The wails and woes of a nation rising up before the walls of Ramah.

Old Samuel sat within the walls of the tiny village. He was not playing piano in Rick's cafe. His bloodshot eyes were scanning the pages of the Torah. His aged hands carefully placed scrolls in the Ark of the Covenant. Soon he would mount his camel and judge cases in small villages from Dan to Beersheba.

Samuel was tormented by the disobedience of Saul, who had snubbed the God of Israel. It seemed like only yesterday that he had waylaid the young Benjamite warrior Saul, and anointed him with oil. Saul had been ferocious in his get-tough policy against Israel's enemies. Yet, sadly, his sword proved sharper than his brain. Like a naughty first-grader he disobeyed the orders of God. He put a price on grey-haired Samuel's head, and the old man fled the Oval Office headquarters of Saul at Gibeah.

The whole experiment in kingship had been a massive blunder. Samuel felt responsible. He had crowned Saul and anointed him with God's spirit. The cries of the people scaled the walls of Ramah. A new king must be found. Samuel brooded in wordless misery at his blighted land's plight. Thoughts of kingship later given voice by poet John Keats reflect Samuel's own musings:

Kings are like starts — they rise and set,
they have the worship of the world
but no repose.

The crown sat heavily on Saul's head. The job was too much for him. The kingmaker Samuel would have to weave the face of a new king in the tangled web that was his soul.

God's spirit at last spoke to speechless Samuel. He and a few servants mounted their camels and set off for a little village called Bethlehem. The City of Bread. The city of Ruth and Boaz. The city where Jesse had grown rich through his vast pasture and flocks of sheep and cattle.

Samuel and his entourage arrived in town on market day. The bleat of sheep, the squawk of geese, and the chirps of hens heralded their arrival. Samuel was viewed as the holiest man in Israel. His arrival in a city was an important event. Townspeople quickly gathered around the bearded prophet. He announced that the reason he had come to town was to offer a sacrifice to the Lord. He asked Jesse and his sons to first come forward and offer their sacrifices. This was a ruse. His real reason for stopping in Bethlehem was to anoint Israel's next King.

Jesse's first son passed before Samuel and was not anointed. Samuel had stayed his own gnarled fingers from pouring the sacred horn's myrrh and cinnamon mixture on the brawny lad. All seven of the boys passed by Samuel without being chosen.

Samuel asked Jesse if he had any more sons. Jesse, the tenth century B.C. version of a Ben Cartwright, owner of a Ponderosa of plenty, told Samuel of his youngest son. A brawny lad named David. A shepherd who fought lions and bears to protect Jesse's extensive flocks. Little did David know he would soon kill enemies to protect Israel's national sheepfold. Soon the star of David would rise above the horizon of hope and beam down on an enlightened land of peace and prosperity.

David knelt before Samuel and in a solemn ceremony was anointed King of Israel. The ceremony was secret and King Saul kept his power. Only in time would it become clear who was the real man to rule God's people.

Some of the eight candidates in the 1984 Democratic New Hampshire primary hoped that the voters of that snowy state would pluck them out of the political chicken fight and anoint them to battle the Goliath in the White House. The chances of this happening proved to be non-existent. We live in a world where the race seems to go to the fleet of foot. The gold medals of wealth and fame are handed out to few. It seems as if the big and powerful rule the roost. It seems as if the prophecy of Big Brother in George Orwell's *1984* is true, and perhaps the symbol of our age should be a warrior smashing in the face of a weak child. In a globe of Davids and Goliaths, the Goliaths usually grab the gold. The Kremlinites crush the Afghans. The rich get the Ritz and the poor get the government cheese. The "hit squads" of Central America are a sober political reality of the day.

This is why I find this tale so fascinating. It reminds me of the young lad Arthur pulling Excaliber out of the stone. It is like Cinderella being chosen at the ball. It is as if the summons had gone out from Moscow for a village lad in distant Siberia to take charge of the Politburo, in the wake of the death of Andropov. It is an incredible story. Almost a fairy tale. Almost as if Samuel should shout out:

Little boy blue come blow your horn!
The sheep's in the meadow, the cow's in the corn.
Where's the boy that looks after the sheep?
He's under the haystack, fast asleep.

In this season of Epiphany we celebrate the birth of him who was anointed in agony and born in a despised province of a hated land. A Son of David born in the village of the shepherd king of old. Christ's birth was heralded by three wise men and not just one wise sage named Samuel. A King anointed with oil even as the young shepherd lad was, in that Bethlehem market place so long ago.

Miracles do happen. God takes the lowly and raises their spirits as high as rainbows. He guides the destinies of people and nations. He gives an ancient people a poet, soldier, and singer named David. He gives us hope that freedom's torch will be kept burning in our black age. He gives us faith that leaders will be found in our church and land. He gives us faith to be led forward by him who is the shepherd of us all, even the Lord Jesus Christ, that great shepherd of the sheep.

First Encounters   *1 Samuel 16:14-23*

Proper 5 (June 5-11)

"Dr. Livingstone, I presume?" were Henry Stanley's opening words to David Livingstone on the shores of Lake Tangayika. "And now, here's Johnny." Ed McMahon's basso profoundo's opening chord in a Carson opus begun over two decades ago, on the *Tonight* show.

First encounters are close encounters of the most important kind. Boswell meeting Dr. Johnson. W. S. Gilbert's lyrics meeting Arthur Sullivan's music. And what would the line be without Mason's encounter with Dixon? Without his partner, Richard Rogers would have had to sing Oklahoma without the sound of music supplied by Oscar Hammerstein. It is hard to think of Simon without Garfunkel; the AFL without the CIO. Harley without Davidson, and Rolls without Royce.

A hefty volume could be scribbled chronicling the first meetings of famous people. The Bible tells of the first time King Saul gazed on the ruddy teenager with muscles of steel and a voice as lilting as a nightingale's. A young lad named David, whose name means "the beloved" had been brought to his humble fortress in Gibeah, a few miles north of Jerusalem. It was a meeting which the old King would never forget. A meeting which would introduce the country bumpkin shepherd to the world of court intrigue and the unsavoury pastime of jockeying for power.

Once, on a lecture tour of America, Oscar Wilde became so disgusted with a reporter who plagued his every step that he retorted, "I never forget a face, but in your case I'll make an exception." Saul never forgot David's face. Even when he tried to kill him with a spear, and even when his KGB thugs tried to murder him, Saul loved David.

Eli Weisel, the brilliant author and a survivor of the Nazi death camps, notes the chief difference between Saul and David. Weisel comments that Saul had to fight enemies within his own soul, while David kept his enemies from entering the citadel of his soul. All of his foes came from without. Were he alive today, King Saul would probably be on a psychiatrist's couch, plagued by King Lear phobias.[1]

Saul was a brilliant warrior. On the eve of battle with the Turks in Palestine, a British major was reading his Bible by a flickering candle. He read in 1 Samuel 13 how the Israelites under Saul's son Jonathan had crept through two sharp rocks to ambush the sleeping Philistines at Micmash. Unbelievably, this is where his own army was. A British brigade slipped through the identical rocks called Bozez and Seneh, overpowered the Turkish guards and routed the enemy. Saul's guerilla tactics worked in the tenth century B.C., worked for the British in 1918, and are still studied today for their tactical genius. Yet for all of his military and political success, Saul is a tragic figure. Saul killed Saul. He committed suicide on Mount Gilboa, but before that he was already spiritually dead. His enemies were in his head. Beset by doubts about himself; possessed by jealousy and disobedience; having a paranoid fear of his lieutenants, his theme might well have been, "wasted days and wasted nights." Old King Cole was a merry old soul, but old King Saul was a tragic monarch. Like Cole, King Saul called for his pipes and he called for his fiddlers three. Unlike Cole, he was not cheered by their melody. By chance, one of his courtiers mentioned a lad from Bethlehem who was skilled at playing the lyre, which we would call an eight-stringed harp. Saul's pony express man arrived at Bethlehem.

Only a few weeks had passed since Samuel had secretly anointed David. Now God's plan of making David the king was getting under way in earnest. Like Saul, David had not had

[1] Weisel, *Five Biblical Portraits,* University of Notre Dame Press, South Bend, Indiana, 1981, chapter on Saul: pp. 69-95.

to fight to achieve power. He was as innocent as his mother's milk. Now God would be working out his purpose of having this bucolic bard replace the wicked and worldly old king. The pony express rider told David he was wanted for a "gig." He was to sing and play lullabies for Saul. Later, Bach would write his brilliant "Goldberg Variations" for a rich patron who wanted him to quiet his nerves at bedtime. But then Bach had not even practiced his scales. David was scaling the charts of fame as he starred in all the local clubs. His voice had soothed the bleat of sheep, while his lyre had struck up a jolly tune for maidens' dancing feet.

God was with the shepherd meeting the sovereign. God is with the Daniel in all of our souls facing the lions of worry, loneliness, and death. He was with his Son in his first encounter with Pilate and the cross of suffering.

David came to Gibeah to meet Saul. The first act in a drama filled with triumph and tragedy. He came to Saul at his request, not because he sought power, but because God's power and mysterious ways had sought him.

It is hard to draw a moral from their meeting; hard to sew up such a complex relationship between such giants as Saul and David in a short chapter. Perhaps it will help if we recognize that all meetings between human beings are important. Remember, too, that it is important to treat all people as children of God, that whom we meet may be planned by God, and that if we can meet Jesus Christ, we can be strengthened for future testing. Future tempests will not defeat us. We have met the weakened lamb hanging from a cross. In his weakness we have discovered his strength. The strength of agape love.

Sticks and Stones   *I Samuel 17:41-48*

Goliath slew David. The boy's bubble of life burst. For twelve years he had lived in a bubble built by doctors to prevent disease from assaulting his body, which lacked immunity to any disease. Recently David died in a Houston hospital room. Hospital staff had come to love him. Doctors meeting the press wept openly. A retired gift shop lady said to a reporter that David had come to be thought of as their own boy by the entire city of Houston. Houston mourns his passing.

It always seems to those who scan the headlines that it is the Goliaths who pound the Davids into the ground. It does seem as if nice guys finish last.

The good news for today is that once upon a time in a land far away, David slew Goliath. Goliath was an early version of Mr. T., and his "A Team" was ready for action. He was the mightiest of Philistines.

The Philistines probably came from the Aegean area of the Mediterranean. Archaeologists have discovered from the black and red artistic pottery of the Philistines that they had been influenced by the culture of Greece. We also know that they were beer guzzlers of enormous proportions — they even had filters in their drinking cups to prevent the barley grains used to brew their beer from sticking in their throats.

The Philistines were great seamen. The Egyptians called them the sea people. Like later day Vikings, they plundered everywhere from the gold mines of Tarsus to the coast of Israel. Today the word Palestine can be traced back to the word Philistine.

About two hundred years before David took on Goliath, the Philistines settled in Israel in the south coastal region, and they established five cities: Ashkelon, Ashdod, Gath,

Ekron, and Gaza. The bellicose Philistines were a powerfully governed people and were culturally more sophisticated than the Hebrews. They were the first to use iron for weapons and the construction of chariots. They were eager to move eastward and sweep the country clean of anyone who would stand in their powerful way. Occasionally a guerilla Robin Hood leader would destroy one of their temples as Samson did at Gaza, or occasionally a mighty warrior like Saul would win a battle. But as the years went on, Philistine power and wealth grew.

Our tale opens in the valley of Elah, about fifteen miles from Jerusalem. A mighty Philistine army was preparing for battle against Saul. Jesse's three sons had joined the army. David was ordered by his father to take his older brothers a luncheon of cheese, flat cakes of bread, and parched corn. David traveled from Bethlehem and reached the Israeli camp. His older brother Eliab promptly scoffed at his offer to fight.

It seems that for forty days Goliath had challenged the best warrior in Israel's camp to single combat. This is a concept foreign to us, but quite common in the works of Homer and other ancient historians. An idea that George Patton revived when he suggested that he and the Desert Fox, Erwin Rommel, duel to the death in tanks under the broiling sun of the North Africa Desert.

Word reached Saul of the young shepherd lad's appearance in the camp. He was the same boy who made trips to Gibeah to serenade Saul when the king was depressed. He summoned David, and in a last-ditch effort to defeat the Philistines, outfitted the shepherd lad in his personal suit of armor. A skilled Jewish tailor from the lower east side of the Bronx would have been helpful, because the armor did not fit David. Or else he did not want it because he was more comfortable with a simple slingshot and a few stones. He explained to Saul that he had killed bears and lions with his expert marksmanship using the sling and stone. Saul acquiesced to the style in which David preferred to fight, and let him out into the "O.K. Corral" between the two armies for the fight to the finish.

Picture the scene: Goliath of Gath standing well over seven feet tall. Probably a descendant of the native Anakite people of Hebron. Able to sympathize with Kareem Abdul Jabbar's remark in his new autobiography that no one loves a Goliath. Like a dragon in a fairy tale, eager to demolish the latest version of St. George. Hear him as he bursts out in a rumbly bass, "Fe fi fo fum! I smell the blood of Jesse's son: Be he alive or be he dead, I'll grind his bones to make my bread."

Goliath taunted David. Told him his young flesh would soon become a vulture burger. David shouted back that he would lop off Goliath's skyscraping head. David aimed well and the stone struck the giant in the forehead. Like Paul Bunyan cutting down a tree, the sound of Goliath's fall resounded in the still valley of Elah. Soon a deafening roar cascaded through the valley of the shadow of death. Goliath's head was buried in Jerusalem, as all of Israel cheered. Legend has it that his big skull was used as a place of execution, and it was on the skull of Goliath that Christ was later crucified.

What's it all about, Alfie? What lifts this story from the Grimm Brothers' fairy tale myth into profound theology? The answer to this question cannot be confined to a few brief words. Perhaps it tells us that whenever God's people are battered and bruised, all is not lost. Perhaps it hints that when the Goliaths of death and despair and grief are about to overwhelm us, there comes to us one like David. The Son of David who defeated the Goliath of grief on an old rugged cross. His name is Jesus. Like David, he is a good shepherd. He defends his people against the bears and the lions who prowl around his flocks scattered throughout earthly meadows.

As the Israel guerilla warriors trusted in a young shepherd named David in the valley of the shadow of death, we too trust in him who walks with us and talks with us along life's busy way. "He lives, he lives, salvation to impart. You ask me how a know he lives, he lives within my heart."

A Hissing Hot Coal   *1 Samuel 18:6-8*

Envy is a hissing hot coal from hell's hearth. Envy waves her wand and a prince savagely surveys a shepherd's success. A shepherd who is also a soldier. A harpist who has become a hero. A popular peasant who has climbed the Everest of adversity.

The king's eyes are so emerald with envy that his pupils resemble shamrocks. Like a Fourth of July watermelon, he is green on the outside, while red with rage on the inside. His envious *eau de cologne* is as fragrant as a convention of Limburger cheese salesmen. He is like those envious blind men described by Dante in *The Purgatorio*, men so blinded by envy that their eyelids have been sewn together for all eternity as punishment.

The final vote has been cast in the primary, and the king has been crushed by a young upstart. Like a tidal wave spitting with foamy fury at the coastline, this lad David has been spewed down the throat of Saul. Saul has been made to swallow the boy's success. He has as much trouble doing so as I experience when gulping down a liver sandwich.

George Balanchine, the founder of the New York City Ballet, instructed his dancers, eager to follow his choreographic genius, to "See the music, hear the dance."

Saul saw the music of the maidens as their dancing feet beat out a tune of triumph. He heard the dance of the prancing priests celebrating victory over the once invincible Philistines. He heard the dance beat out in a rhythmic tattoo pounded by Him who marched to the beat of a different drummer. For though Saul had slain his thousands, David had slain ten thousands. "Hey, Mr. Tambourine man, sing a song for me." "Hey Sergeant Pepper, pour some salt into the festering wound of envy gripping at Saul's heart." "Hail the conquering hero home from the wars." When David comes marching home, hurrah! hurrah!

Look well into the mirror of Saul. His face is much like our face. We too have envied others and nursed jealousy at the breast of our being. We too have had to confess that we have sung the dirge wrung from Mephisto's heart in Christopher Marlowe's *Faust*:

> *Why this is hell*
> *Think . . . that I who saw the face of God*
> *and tasted the eternal Joys of heaven*
> *Am not tormented with ten thousand hells*
> *In being deprived of everlasting bliss?*

Like Mephisto and Saul, we too have known the ten thousand hells of envy. If greed is the sin of the "haves" against the "have-nots," then envy, the hellish greeneyed siren, is the sin of the "have-nots" against that gaggle of guys and gals with oomph, charisma, and cash.

Envy is deadly, silent, and universal. Like glaucoma, it destroys our eyesight. Like Topsy it just grows. Like crabgrass it insults him who leads us into green pastures. It is a feeling most of us will not even admit to having stored away in some Swiss account of malice in the soul's bank. There are telltale signs that it is alive and well in us.

I am an envier. I am a confessed clergybird who flies in a flock of prima donna pulpiteers. Together we shall briefly explore how to spot envy on our radar screens, in hopes we can shoot it out of the friendly skies.

A squirrel once said to a mountain, "You may carry a forest on your back, but you can't store acorns in safe places like I can." If we followed the advice of that squirrel, perhaps we would not be so "squirrely" ourselves.

The hymn puts it rather bluntly "Count your blessings, count them one by one." Learn to rejoice in the success and victories of others. Remember too that all that glitters is not gold. Even the rich, famous, and talented have troubles that perhaps you aren't forced to deal with. Count your "lucky stars" that God has blessed you in many ways — ways so taken for granted and so often forgotten. If everyone in that often envious flock called the church would use what talents God has given them, think what could be accomplished. As Christians, our role is to count our blessings on the abacus of agape love, as we forget self and remember the Savior. He who had no money, no home, no friends, and no chance in a rough-and-tumble world. He who is the Christ, and who died since, as Matthew put it, they put him on the cross because the priests and big-shots were envious of him.

In an ancient cemetery behind a church building in Hatfield, Massachusetts, is this epitaph found on a mouldering tombstone:

> Beneath this stone, a lump of clay
> Lies Arabella Young
> Who on the 21st of May
> Began to hold her tongue.

Let us hold our tongues of clacking jealousy. Let us use those tongues to rejoice in praise of Him who has given us talents, blessings, and opportunities, to serve him who is the Son of David and Son of God — even Jesus the Christ.

Three Arrows   *1 Samuel 20:18-23*

We follow flights of arrows. We watch for them at inter-sections. We pursue them with haste as we speed our carts down supermarket aisles. We follow them up staircases at work, and down bleacher steps at the basketball gym. When we want to win friends and influence people, we males can often be found with an Arrow shirt on our backs. Females of the species are hopeful some gentleman will aim Cupid's arrow at their hearts.

We forget that arrows were once weapons. Archaeologists have dug up more arrows in the land of Israel than Quaker has oats.

David and Jonathan knew about arrows. They were both brave warriors who had fought against the Philistines. Jonathan was the son of King Saul, and David's best friend. The story of David and Jonathan is a story of friendship at its best. Aristotle said that a friend can be defined as a single soul dwelling in two bodies. No wonder then that we read that Jonathan loved David as his own soul. Even as the Son of David would love a disciple named John, did David love Jonathan.

Mark Twain once told a reporter, "I don't say much about heaven and hell because I have friends in both places." David's heavenly friendship with Jonathan took place in the crucible of Saul's hellish jealousy. Saul hated David because of his popularity and his prowess as a warrior. He reminded Jonathan that this upstart from Bethlehem might even become the next king and usurp his role as the crown prince awaiting the throne.

Jonathan often risked his life to warn David of danger. To Jonathan's way of thinking, the power of friendship was stronger than the Machiavellian quest for power. He had already told David to flee during a black day when the melancholy monarch Saul wished to murder the shepherd lad.

Now, as the feast of the new moon was approaching, the two lads met in a field. In this meeting under the open sky they were safe from the prying ears of spies. They met to reaffirm their covenant of friendship, and devised a test to see if David should continue in Saul's court. David suggested to Jonathan that he leave the king's table for a few days. Israel's kings usually ate with only their closest advisors. In Saul's case, he dined with his son Jonathan, his general Abner, and his lyre player, David. No women were allowed at his table, as is still the custom with Middle Eastern sheiks.

While David hid in the valley of Ezel, Saul noticed his absence on the first day of the feast. "Perhaps he is ritually unclean and so is not with me," reasoned Saul. On the second day of his absence, Jonathan suggested that David had returned home to offer sacrifices with his family. Saul was furious — to think that David would not appear at his table. In fury he even threw a spear at Jonathan.

On the morning of the third day, Jonathan and a young archer went to the field where David was hiding by a big rock. Earlier they had planned as a signal the use of three arrows. If the arrows shot by the archer landed in front of the rock, then David knew the coast was clear and he could return to Saul's court in safety. If, however, the arrows were shot over the rock, David was to flee for his life. The arrows flew through the spring air and arched their message of flight over the fugitive hovering behind the rock pile — David was to run for his life.

He emerged from the rock, salaamed three times before Jonathan, and the two men kissed each other. Then they parted only to meet once more in the barren wilderness near Arabia.

David would later bury Jonathan after his death in battle against the Philistines. He would never forget the friendship of Jonathan, and would see to it that the lame son of his friend always had a place reserved for him at his table.

The friendship of David and Jonathan was as strong as Gibraltar; as everlasting as the waves beating on the shores, and as fragrant as an April garden caressed by a midmorning rain.

The shepherd was seized by raiders and became a slave. Each day he would call his sheep by name, and legend has it, that he even talked to the birds and played melodies to them with his flute. Legend insists that this shepherd of peace drove out the serpents of his new land. His name was St. Patrick.

The shepherd we worship had not read Dale Carnegie and the pop psychologists who exhort us on effective methods enabling us to "win friends and influence people." He had no friends on that black Friday night of betrayal. Christ, who is the friend of us all, died friendless and despised. The Son of David, who is the friend of the fugitives and the forsaken. The Good Shepherd who brings comfort and love to the prisoner.

In the days given to him before his execution by the Nazis, Dietrich Bonhoeffer, the young German pastor, wrote these words from his prison cell in Tegel:

> *Who am I?*
> *restless and longing and sick,*
> *like a bird in a cage.*
> *struggling for breath, as though*
> *hands were compressing my throat,*
> *yearning for colors, for flowers,*
> *for the voices of birds,*
> *thirsting for words of kindness,*
> *for neighbors.*[1]

Jonathan was a friend to David in the shepherd's dark night of the soul. A friend is someone who is at your doorstep when the rest of the world has gone home. Proverbs 18:24 speaks of a friend who sticks to us closer than death. His name is Jesus Christ. Because of his friendship for us, we are empowered to reach out our hands in friendship to other people.

[2] Dietrich Bonhoeffer, *Prayers From Prison*, "Who am I? Fortress Press, Philadelphia, 1979, p. 17.

April Showers   *1 Samuel 20:18-23*

"Raindrops keep falling on my head." A line not limited to the bluesy baritone of B. J. Thomas. We have all sung the blues in April. T. S. Eliot, writing in the disillusioned years after World War 1, lamented:

April is the cruelest month
breeding lilacs out of the dead land
mixing memory and desire
stirring dull roots with spring rain.

The Ides of April demand a wampum payment to our rich uncle in Washington. Except for a dynamic duo in the N.C.A.A. basketball championship game, a nation of basketball fans are singing a dirge about, "Wait until next year." Our east coast lies battered and broken in the wake of stormy fury. Though April showers may bring May flowers, that does not help much when you stand sopping wet in the middle of a cold Ohio Valley spring. The word "April" comes from the Latin word *aperio* meaning "to open." The Romans observed April when the technicolor cast of thousands of flowers raised their pastel colored heads upward toward the blue Italian skies.

Spring was once observed as the new year. In many lands April first was New Year's Day. Not until Pope Gregory I decreed January first to be New Year's Day did April cease to be viewed as the beginning of a new year.

April may be cruel but it can also be a clarion call to a new creation. A month of crucifixion can be a month of empty tombs and reports of resurrection. April, like any month, can be what we make of it.

David had slain his ten thousands; he had had his Paul Newman blue eyes on the cover of *Time* and *People*. He had married the boss's daughter and had become the best friend of the next lad in line for the lionship of Judah.

Then his newly won fame and glory turned as rotten as a Dead Sea orange. The hero became a fugitive. A Robin Hood bandit. A guerilla warrior skulking in the shadows of caves and Clorox-bleached rocks down by the Dead Sea. His plight of flight wasn't an optimistic way to sail into a new year, be it in January or April.

Early in the spring he was hiding in the wilderness of Ziph, just four or so miles away from Hebron. Suddenly a friend approached the camp. Longfellow said that friends are "way stations of love on life's journey." Jonathan was such a friend to David. Jonathan simply said to David, "Fear not! Saul, my angry father, won't harm you. I will help you. I will gladly give up my right to the throne and be your best friend. Your fear shall not defeat you. Your friend shall be to you closer than a brother."

That was the last time David looked on the face of his friend. Soon the cries of warriors would drown out Jonathan's gentle words of love. The stench of mouldering corpses slain in hot fight would cover the fragrant cologne of courage which Jonathan gave to David that spring morning.

Yet David, like the phoenix, would arise out of the ashes of Job-like despair. He would take courage from Jonathan's friendship. He would wrestle with his fear and emerge from the contest with the triumph. Homer's heroes — Achilles, or Ajax, or even Nestor, never show fear. Yet the Bible dares assert that the Lion of the tribe of Judah — the greatest warrior in Israeli history was scared out of his wits in the desert.

Centuries before Freud, the court historian who wrote our story knew that one of the most basic human emotions in a crisis is fear. Yet, like a leitmotiv in a Wagnerian opera, the words FEAR NOT conquer the minor key of despair, and rise to a crescendo of victory throughout the holy text.

Mark Twain remarked, "I am an old man and have known many troubles — most of them never happened."

Our age of anxiety crafts worry warts and plants them in the gardens of our souls. Unlike *Mad's* Alfred E. Newman, few of us can blithely say, "What, me worry?"

This is what Jonathan told David. That is what John the Baptizer said to a people in the wilderness. He told them that the Son of David would come and that their worries about the coming of the Messiah would drown like a sparrow in the sea.

Fear knocked on the door; faith answered; there was no one there. Faith is not a fancy Sunday go-to-meeting gentleman dismissed with the dispatch of a Sunday dinner.

Alexander Maclaren, the doughty Scot, said faith to him was a visitor,

> *... When we are afraid ... we trust in God not in easy times when things are going smoothly with us. Not when the sun shines but when the tempest blows and the wind howls about his ears ... The midnight sea lies all black. And so it is from the tumults and agitations of man's spirit that there is struck the light of faith. What time I am afraid, I will trust.*[1]

David had a lot of faults but this shepherd never tried to pull the wool over the eyes of the Good Shepherd.

The Son of David, who was prefect love, was afraid one black night in Gethsemane's garden. He had no Jonathan to comfort him. He prayed, alone and abandoned by his friends and each of us. Nothing on the morrow would ease his troubled brow. He would be executed. No wonder that in Gethsemane's ancient garden he asked the Ancient of Days to remove the cup of suffering from his hands.

Silence met his pleas. He drank the cup of death, defeat, and degradation to the bitter dregs. He died so that Death and his henchman Fear would beat against the island of our mortality and be stayed in their fury by his defenceworks of love.

[1] Alexander Maclaren, *Week-Day Evening Addresses,* Funk & Wagnells Co., New York, 1902, p. 104.

At church we sing silently with our choir the old chant about him who is our friend, him who conquers our fears and steadies our boat as we sail into the cruelest month of all. Can you catch the melody of Katherine Tynan on the evening breeze?

All in the April evening
April airs were abroad
The sheep with their little lambs
passed me on the road
The lambs were weary and crying
With a weak human cry

I thought on the Lamb of God
going meekly to die
Up on a hilltop green
Only a cross of shame
Two stark crosses between
All in the April evening.

I saw the sheep with their lambs
and thought on the Lamb of God.[2]

[2] "All In the April Evening," Theodore Presser Company, Bryn Mawr, Pennsylvania, 1910.

Cameos of Conscience   1 Samuel 22:1-19

To Tell the Truth. Which of the three contestants is the real McCoy? The climactic moment when the host commands the true-bluer to stand.

Standing up for truth is easier on game shows than it is in life. Telling the truth does not always set you free. Truth telling can be as joyous as a summons to the IRS office. As painful as a dentist's drill driving deep into your molar with purring fury. Truth's consequences are often as dark as a Harlan County mine. Because telling the truth is so hard, sometimes it becomes like a chocolate drop which melts in our mouths. Truth has often been shanghaied into boarding a "Good Ship Lollipop" that has been populated by a crew of sugar-coated syllables.

Ahimelech told the truth, so help him God. His crime was helping a fugitive. A rag-tag Robin Hood singing a sad song of flight, "Down every road there's always one more city, I'm on the run, the highway is my home," knowing full well the despair evoked in Merle Haggard's lament.

David running in fear from Saul. One morning, entering into the sleepy village of Nob, nestled on Mount Scopus, a few miles from Jerusalem. Making up a story. Telling a lie. Informing Ahimelech, the high priest, that he is on a secret mission for Saul. Begging the priest to feed him with the sacred bread, to keep his men and himself alive. Well-fed and blessed by Ahimelech, David slips out of the sun-drenched village to fight another day. A fox on the run from the hounds of hate unleashed by Saul.

Doeg, the most obedient of Saul's dogs, is at Nob. Perhaps he is there at the holy hamlet to be cleansed from his leprosy. He returns to Saul and tells him that David has received help from the priest Ahimelech.

Saul bellows blasphemy against the priests of Israel. He smells conspiracy against him in the land. "So the religious bigwigs are with David?" "So the ministerial association has passed a resolution against me?"

The Jekyll of goodness in Saul's being has given up the ghost. The Mr. Hyde of malice and murder has arisen like a tidal wave, beating with fury against a helpless city. The king's storm troopers disturbed the peace of Nob. Ahimelech and eighty-four priests were brought before the king as he sat in judgment under a sacred tree.

Ahimelech tells his story. David had lied to him, but the priest still did not know this. He tells Saul with honesty that he had fed David because he was starving. He tells Saul that David was his most loyal captain. Saul could not see the truth even though it had been written in letters as large as an eye chart. His nostrils seemed to catch a whiff of conspiracy, as fetid as an overflowing cesspool.

Saul demanded that Ahimelech and his fellow priests be put to the sword. None of his storm troopers would kill the men of God before his throne. The breeze gently caught the tamarisk tree's attention. The sun gleamed with yellow gold on the heavy swords of his troopers. Like lambs presented for the slaughter, Ahimelech stood as his heart beat a macabre march of death.

At last the sound of silence was extinguished with the fall of a sword blade. Doeg and his men cut down the innocent Ahimelech.

The first holocaust against the people of Israel was begun by her first king. "Holocaust" comes from two Greek words. "Holo" meaning "whole" and "caust" meaning "burnt." A holocaust is a burnt offering to God. Soon the town of Nob was the victim of a holocaust. All of the women, children, and cattle were destroyed. Only Abiathar the son of Ahimelech survived the bloodbath, as he escaped to David: at the cave of Adullam by the barren shore of the Dead Sea.

To most of us this tale about the death of Ahimelech is obscure. Jesus, though, knew the tale well. Once he told a conclave of Pharisees that he remembered how David had received a gift of showbread, sacred bread to feed his starving guerilla band. Jesus said that Ahimelech gave it to David on the Sabbath. It would be as if someone banged open the white doors of your church one Sunday and begged you to feed him your communion bread.

Jesus was commending Ahimelech for putting compassion for the stranger above ceremony. Ahimelech dared to tell the truth as he saw that truth. The truth was that he was not in rebellion against Saul. The truth was that, because of his kindness to David, he had to die in the murderous grip of a tyrant.

Because he bandaged the wounded John Wilkes Booth, an innocent Dr. Samuel Mudd served long years of imprisonment. Because Martin Niemoller had the audacity to stand up in the most prestigious Lutheran pulpit in Berlin and shout to the rafters, "Not you, Adolf Hitler, but Jesus Christ is my Fuhrer," this Iron Cross hero of World War I had to bear a cross of suffering in Dachau.

Emily Dickinson, the gentle New England recluse, advised us to tell the truth with a slant. Sometimes the bare-boned truth can hurt others and needs sugar-coating to make it easier to swallow.

But an outright lie is a spearthrust into the heart of him who is the Way, the Truth, and the Life.

From Nob to Nob Hill men and women have had to suffer for the crime of loving others and trying to live innocent and peaceful lives. From the Death Squads of El Salvador to the bloody scorched earth of the Middle East, innocent children cry in the night of death. Our suffering century of holocaust horror has erected millions of crosses on countless Calvarys. We have lied and cheated in our mad quest for power. Our polluted lives and skies have blotted out the sun of love.

Today I urge you to look to the Man for All Seasons for forgiveness and courage. Courage to tell the truth and to proclaim the truth of him who is the Truth of Love, even Jesus the Christ.

The Farmer and the Fugitive
1 Samuel 25:9-17

"The Lord is my shepherd, I shall want." "The Lord is my shepherd, I shall not want." The bad shepherd; the good shepherd. A miserly master and a merciful master. A Scrooge and a singer of songs. An old farmer and a young warrior. A Prince and a Pauper. A farmer and a fugitive. Nabal and David. Two faces staring at us across the centuries.

The April fool is Nabal. Owner of three thousand sheep and three thousand goats. Married to the prettiest girl in town. Owner of rich pasture lands a few miles south of Hebron. Employer of countless servants who labor for him without benefit of a union contract. A Cadillac cowboy wont to drive his one horsepower stallion down Easy Street. Day after day this fool on a hill counted his coins and surveyed his lands.

One day, ten men who worked for David dropped by to see Nabal. They had been out in the fields protecting Nabal's flocks from sheep rustlers. They were hungry; since there was no McDonald's in the area, they wanted a simple luncheon of bread and wine.

Nabal was furious. The fur hit the fan. The mild April air turned blue with his curses. He shouted out with the loud baritone, a sonic boom, "Shall I take my bread and water and meat and give it to men who are strangers? Send them away at once. My door is closed to them." Need had knocked at the door of hospitality, only to discover that anger had turned it away.

When David heard about the insult to his men he was so angry he wanted to kill the old fool. Anger seems to breed anger. Insults bear an affinity to the Hydra in Greek mythology, who grew heads as soon as you tried to lop one off. Anger is a hydra-headed demon forever lurking in our soul's closet.

Because of his anger, Nabal hurt himself. He took to drink to drown his anger. His family would be torn from his grasp as his wife Abigail came to deplore his rudeness. His employees saw his anger and turned away from him in skulking fear. His anger was a hammer striking the anvil of agony for Nabal and everyone he knew.

David reacted to Nabal's rudeness with anger of his own. He wanted to strike the farmer down with his sharp blade. He wanted to pursue a scorched earth policy and wipe Nabal's farm off the face of the earth.

All of Nabal's troubles started when he said "no" to someone in need. Because he refused the crust of bread to a stranger, all of his power and glory would be taken from him.

Miss Schlegel, a well-heeled aristocrat in E. M. Forster's novel *Howard's End*, says, "You and I stand upon money as islands . . . we ought to remember that we are standing on these islands and that most of the others are down below the surface of the sea."[1] Nabal's "Fantasy Island" existence would sink into the sunset because of his angry rudeness. His decline was imminent because his temper was as explosive as the volcano on the Italian island of Stromboli. Because, like baseball's Billy Martin, he enjoyed kicking water coolers and umpires in the shins, Nabal's path to destruction was broad and open.

Once there was a rich land owner in Virginia. A biographer tells us that he would receive about a thousand visitors a year — some of them staying at his farm for several weeks or even months. His farm was often in debt, and he had to find shillings to feed the constant Coxey's army of callers who dropped in on him. This wealthy plantation owner turned no one away from the table at Mount Vernon. George Washington's door was always open to those in need.

Nabal's door was always closed as tight as his fists around gold coins. Benjamin Disraeli once said of an

---

[1] E. M. Forster, *Howard's End,* Random House, New York, p.61.

opponent, "He is a self-made man and worships himself." That was Nabal in a nutshell. He worshiped his C.D.'s in the bank and gave to charity only when it would mean a tax break on his ledgers. He was as coldhearted as a convention of icicles in Alaska.

The great preacher Studdert-Kennedy said that Easter is popular but Lent is not. Lent is the agony, while Easter is the ecstacy. Perhaps one reason Lent is not popular is because it is a mirror. Perhaps, when we gaze into it, we do not discover the face of a risen Christ, but our own faces. Mark Twain wrote that we are all moons because we have a dark side we do not want anyone to see.

Nabal was so foolish that all of us can see his rude and insulting nature with the clearness of a highpowered microscope. In this story most of us side with the good guys who had the door slammed in their faces. Perhaps we would do well to associate ourselves with Nabal. Like him, all of us have let the sun go down on our anger. Anger is not always a sin. After all, Jesus was often angry with fat cats stealing cheese from poor church mice. The anger the Bible says is foolish is the emotion that puts the lid on compassionate love. Anger that destroys ourselves, our families, and our friends.

Rich men, and even nice middle class folk, for the most part shut the door in the Son of David's face. There was no room for him at the inn. No room for him in the Temple, where his disciples might place their muddy feet on the new church carpet. No room for him anywhere except on a cross of shame.

Like Nabal, we have so often shut Christ out of our lives. Like him we have turned the stranger away from our doors. Like him we often worship things and value them more than people.

Today, we confess our angers and our insults. Today, we are called to remember and confess those unguarded moments when we have cast aspersions on others. Today we are to confess our failure to cast out nets of love and understanding.

The hope of Lent is that the crucified Christ died not only for the meek and mild, but for the Nabals and the Judases as well. With Nabal, and all the black-hatted band of baddies in the Bible, we stand at the foot of the cross, confessing our sins and looking to Christ for redemption. With Isaac Watts we sing:

> When I survey the wondrous cross
> on which the Prince of Glory died
> My richest gain I count but loss
> And pour contempt on all my pride. [2]

[2] "When I Survey the Wonderous Cross," *Worship Book of the Presbyterian Church,* Westminster Press, Philadelphia, 1973.

Bound for Glory   *1 Samuel 25:29-31*

Beauty and the Beast. The beastly brute is Nabal. A grumpy geezer. A gentleman farmer whose grasp for gold was only exceeded by his grasp for Mogen David. His eyes gazed over the greenly robed spring fields as he saw his herds of sheep gently grazing. His ears heard the bleat of sheep as nine pounds of wool was removed from their fat lamb shoulders. His nose caught the fragrant smell of rich foods placed on his teeming table by servants forced to work for a Simon Legree whip-cracking master.

A few miles south of Hebron in the tiny village of Maon, Nabal had carved out an empire of land, livestock, and lucre. All was "hunkey-dorey" until David proved to be the fly in the ointment.

It happened during the sheep shearing festival of an emerald green springtime. Ten of David's men asked for food and drink at Nabal's ranch. David and his 600 followers were operating a "protection agency." To protect the lands of the farmers in the area, they expected to be wined and dined and given enough money to live, as they nestled in the caves near the Dead Sea. The churlish Nabal, whose name in Hebrew means "a fool," refused them hospitality and told David's warriors to vamoose off his property pronto. When David heard of this insult he was furious. Filled with anger, he vowed to slaughter not only Nabal, but everyone on his farm, all of his family and servants and sheep: even the entire village of Maon.

David and Nabal. Two strong men about to collide in a furious life-and-death struggle. Two roaring lions of rage growling for an easy kill.

Suddenly, there enters into the story a young woman whose name is Abigail. Abigail was the beauty married to the beast Nabal. She ordered five of her prettiest servants to saddle up the donkeys with 200 fig cakes, 200 loaves of bread fresh from the bakery, and ten whole cooked sheep — enough to provide a lamb chop dinner fit for even the kingly appetite of David.

Tradition has it that these maidens wore low-cut blouses with skirts split up to the waist, heavy makeup, and gossamer-thin veils over their stately heads. Abigail and her party met David as he was leading his camelmounted band licketysplit down the mountain which led to the ranch. Abigail quickly jumped down from her donkey which she rode as a symbol of humbleness and peace. She fell before David, kissed his feet, and begged him to spare her fool of a husband. David's eye was already soothed by the five beauties she had brought with her. He was deeply moved by Abigail's plea for mercy. His heart was stirred when she told him that his vengeance could fall on her if he would only spare everyone else.

Abigail Smith tried to keep peace between her headstrong father and her impertinent lover. Dealing with her boyfriend was not easy. After all, here is a sample of one of his love letters:

> *Dear Madam, I enclose a catalogue of your faults, imperfections and defects. You can't sing, you are unable to play cards and you walk with your toes turned inward.*

This Abigail had a tart tongue and could hold her own in a heated discussion with her beau. Her father, a Congregational minister, was so upset over his genteel daughter wedding an upstart farmer, that his only consolation was that his daughter would use her sharp tongue to rip asunder the young man's haughty pride, and that her atrocious cooking would starve him into obedient submission. In fact, when the Rev. William Smith performed the wedding service for daughter Abigail and farmer John on October 25, 1764, he preached

[1] Paul F. Boller, Jr., *Presidential Anecdotes*, Penguin Books, 1981, p. 28.

a wedding sermon based on the text (Matthew 11:28), "For John came neither eating or drinking and they said he had a demon." And so our second President, John Adams, wed our second first lady, Abigail Smith Adams.

Back at the ranch, Nabal wondered where his beautiful wife had gone with her beautiful retinue. Abigail at last arrived home and told her husband of her good deed for the day. Abigail heard the denunciations uttered by her mate as he drowned with wine his sorrow and anger at her. Within ten days he was dead of a stroke or heart attack. His anger had killed him. The beautiful widow Abigail soon wed David. David had not let his anger triumph over his kingly soul. He had taken the bundle of life given to him by Abigail.

What did Abigail mean when she told David that his enemies would not defeat him because he was in the bundle of the living? Even today "the bundle of the living" is a phrase often carved on the tombstones of orthodox Jews.

In David's day Samsonite Luggage did not sell many suitcases. People, when traveling, would wrap their most precious possessions in a cloth. The Jews believed that God wraps the souls of all of his children in a bundle as he journeys across creation. The "bundle of life" in Hebrew is *se per hayyin.* Bundle means a book that is bound by ties which bind it together. To fall out of this bundle meant to lose eternal life, to fall into the chaos of hellish darkness and to be forgotten by God.

Later, we Christians used the concept of the "bundle of life" as we developed belief in that roll which will be called up yonder. The "bundle of life" is the Lamb's Book of Life. Abigail was telling David that we are not to let anger and vengeance, Hatfield and McCoy feuds conquer our spirits. We are to let the Lord deal with the nasties and the meanies. Our job is to keep the lid on anger as tightly clasped as a cookie jar is before a Cub Scout meeting.

Nabal was a fool because his anger so upset him that he died from it. David, who was an emotional man with mercurial mood swings, nevertheless was able to bridle his warlike impulses as he remembered that he was indeed in the bundle of life. He was bound for glory, because he was one of God's faithful children. By yielding to hate he would fall out of this bundle and end up in a bundle of black despair and inner darkness.

Do you remember some Abigail who curbed your anger? Have you ever been an Abigail yourself and been a peacemaker in your home, or church, or school, or work? As you read these words, you are in the bundle of life. We are all being carried through the valleys and mountains by the everlasting arms of a loving Father. A Father whose Son on Easter morning broke the strong ties of death, and opened the black tomb to lead us to glory.

The next time you are angry; the next time you help to prevent a donnybrook of hate; or an argument sparked by the flames of gossip, remember that you are in the Lamb's book of life. Remember that because of Christ we can all live as peacemakers. Martin Luther says it well:

> Christ Jesus lay in death's strong bands
> But now at God's right hand he stands
> And brings us life from heaven
> Wherefore let us joyful be
> And sing to God right thankfully
> Loud songs of Alleluia, Alleluia! Amen
> ("Christ Lay in Death's Strong Bonds," 1524)

Battle Cries

2 Samuel 1:25-27

Proper 6 (June 12-18)

Battle cries. "How are the mighty fallen in the midst of battle." "I believe for every drop of rain that falls a newborn baby cries." "When your sweetheart sends a letter of good-bye, let your hair down and give yourself a cry." Cries of pain in the night and flashing ambulance lights. Cries of horror as a bomb hits another frail building in Beirut. Tears pouring down a widow's weatherbeaten face as she gently places flowers on a newly-dug grave.

Battle cries. The mighty and the meek fall in life's battle each day. No son of Adam or daughter of Eve is alien to the dark landscape of grief.

Saul and Jonathan had fallen to the mighty armies of the Philistines. High on the rocky slopes of Mount Gilboa, the flower of a generation had been plucked by the cruel hands of the conqueror. Now the northern territory lay in enemy hands. Now the leaders of the nation had fallen into the abyss of death. Now there was wailing and gnashing of teeth.

The fetid odor of death was wafted southward to David in Ziklag. Saul was dead and the nation had no king. Jonathan was dead and friendship was dead in David's breast. Stars were garbed in black shrouds, the sun was erased from the skies, and the cry of mourning was heard in every home. David was slain by the news of defeat and death. Salty tears gushed down his bronzed and battle-scarred cheeks. His heart was a Dead Sea of sorrow. His pen bled with the anguish of a broken soul as he poured out his pain on paper.

In Flanders field the poppies blow
Between the crosses row on row[1]

---

[1] "In Flanders Field," John McCrae, from *Bartlett's Familiar Quotations*, John Bartlett, ed., Little, Brown, and Company, Boston, 1968, p. 912.

In the Soviet Union twenty million persons died in World War II. Harrison Salisbury of the *New York Times* has written that, in all likelihood, at least one member of every Soviet family fell in that conflict. Recently, droves of Americans visited Normandy where over forty years ago men of the allies paid a terrible price for freedom on D-Day of 1944.

The Argentine reporter Jacobo Timerman writes in *The Longest War, Israel in Lebanon*, of the anguish experienced in the streets of Tel Aviv by parents reading the news of their sons' deaths in Lebanon.

A policewoman's life is snuffed out on a London street by the black puff of a Libyan bomb. A peasant in Nicaragua is found murdered by a death squad. The world is a violent arena of danger. The Rocky Balboas often end up in the corner where Darth Vaders of despair pummel timid spirits into smithereens. A nation mourns and suffers pain as the Kennedy family buries a son.

David's lament for Saul and Jonathan, and for himself, is a song all of us have sung or will sing.

In Flanders field the poppies blow
between the crosses row on row.[2]

In some field perhaps far away from Flanders or Mount Gilboa or Normandy, lies someone for whom you mourn.

Death is a reality we disguise with Victorian propriety. A reality that is as much a part of nature as are the April showers that precede May flowers. David's lament is valuable to us today. It shows us that even the mighty fall and even the mighty cry. Christianity is not stoicism. We Christians cry when we lose someone we love. Stiff upper lips are for prudes and not Presbyterians.

David is a classic example of grief. Yet he recovers. He never forgets his love for Jonathan and his ambivalent

[2] Ibid

feelings towards Saul. He does take the following steps in the grief process. He talks about the dead loved ones and weeps openly. He accepts sympathy from others in the camp who knew Saul and Jonathan and the others who were slain.

The pain of loss does not go away, but with time's passing it does become more bearable. God uses time to heal us. Grief is a season when we need to turn to the Bible, and be refreshed by the living words of the Word. Someone bowed down by death once wrote,

> *I ... looked at a page of Psalms til the wintry sea of trouble was soothed as by summer calms for the words of old seemed new in their power to comfort as they brought me their word of cheer.*

David prayed with his stricken people and continued to praise God, who is Lord over life and death, loss and reunion. When grief bites into life's banquet, we are to continue praying and worshiping him with others. It hurts us to do this, but it also heals us. We are not alone in grief. All of us have worn stripes of suffering in God's army. All of us are wounded warriors in life's battles.

David continued to work. He did not sit in his goats' hair tent and pluck his harp all week. He had an enemy to defeat. A nation to bind together and an empire to secure. Work can help us when grief raps his cold hand on our door.

All nature mourned when the Prince of Glory died upon the tree. God has lost a son, the Son of David, who died so that death would not be ultimately triumphant. Faulkner was right, "Man can be defeated but he can't be destroyed." A dying Peter Marshall whispered to his wife Catherine, "Goodbye — see you in the morning."

Easter morning has dawned. Death has no longer his black dominion over our souls. As the Scottish composer George Matheson would put it,

O Love that wilt not let me go
I rest my weary soul in thee;
I give thee back the life I owe . . .
I trace the rainbow through the rain
And feel the promise is not vain
That morn shall tearless be.
And from the ground that blossoms red
Life that shall endless be. Amen [3]

Christ lives. Hallalujah!

[3] "O Love That Wilt Not Let Me Go," from *Worship Book of the Presbyterian Church,* Westminster Press, Philadelphia, 1973.

Color It Purple

2 Samuel 5:1-12
Proper 7 (June 19-25)

David. A man for all seasons. A minstrel whose songs will be sung as long as vocal chords vibrate in humanity's throat. A happy warrior whose paths of glory saunter across a score of bloody battlefields. A prince of peace who knew, as did General Sherman, that "war is hell." An astute politician whose savvy grasp of statecraft reveal him as a Machiavellian prince of the first rank. An athlete knowing full well what "Wide World of Sports" likes to call "the thrill of victory; the agony of defeat." David: poet, prince, and praise-singer. David: sinner and saint. David. Here was a man.

The Color Purple is Steven Spielberg's film based on Alice Walker's novel about a homely and downtrodden Georgia black woman. In the movie, "purple is a life-giving color symbolic of love and hope."

Marc Chagall in his 1956 lithograph of David, painted the great hero's beard purple. By doing so he was emphasizing the kingly nature of this greatest of Israel's kings. Purple is a bright color. A color of hope. A color of promise. A Messianic color of kingship heralding the coming Christ, whose kingship will color the universe with a crayola of caring, sharing, and daring.

Ralph Waldo Emerson wrote, "The true test of a civilization is not the census, nor the size of the cities . . . but the kind of man the country turns out."

The pygmy-sized fledgling nation of outcasts and slaves called Israel had produced a Goliath of a man when David was born in Bethlehem. A man who would establish a City of Peace on Zion's hill. A man who would give a butterfly of hope and stability to a land racked by bitter civil war and invasion from foreign armies.

Mighty as Macbeth in war; as filled with doubts as Hamlet; as heartbroken by family tragedies as King Lear, David captures our hearts with ease.

Murphy's law proclaims that nothing is easy. Most things take more time than we first think and if anything can go wrong, it will.

A lot of things went wrong in David's seventy years. He saw war and death without benefit of bifocals. He saw God in all his tragedies and triumphs. Will Rogers quipped, "It's great to be great but it's greater to be human." David was great, but in his sin, suffering, and striving, he was also human.

The leaders of the nation came to him at Hebron. David's chief rival for kingship, Ish-bosheth, the last remaining son of Saul, had been murdered. The forces of Saul had been routed by the ruddy-cheeked warriors who wielded the weapons of war in David's cause. Now the promise of David was to be fulfilled by his being granted the sceptre of royal rule.

The elders called David to the throne because of his kinship with them, his military prowess, and their belief it was God calling him to lead his people. David accepted the challenge, and the dynasty linking God, Israel, and David's family became an invulnerable trinity whose glory would become realized in the Messiah — Jesus Christ.

In his commentary, *First and Second Samuel* (Westminster Press, Philadelphia, 1976, p. 266), Hans Wilhelm Hertzberg notes, ". . . the promise to David is fulfilled; he becomes king over all the people, and becomes king in Jerusalem. All that is still to come can only be confirmation, assurance and consequence of this one fact."

While none of us will be called to kingship, all of us will receive collect calls. Somerset Maugham commented, "In heaven when the blessed use the telephone, they will say what they have to say and not a word besides."

The elders came to David in order to collect his energy, intelligence, imagination, and love for the night and day depository of needs called the nation of Israel.

We receive collect calls from friends and family every day. We pay the rent we owe God for the space we occupy, if we respond to those needs with listening ears; kind words and loving embraces. We do so because we love and serve him who is Son of David; Son of God, and our redeemer and friend, Jesus Christ.

Invitation to the Dance   *2 Samuel 6:1-15*

Proper 8 (June 26-July 2)

June is an inviting month. Juno was the Roman goddess who protected women and cared for brides. No wonder June is the favorite month for weddings. June is also a month for graduations and reunions. June is when Stravinsky's "Rites of Spring" are muted, while Gershwin's "Summertime and the Living is Easy" tune floats like a monarch butterfly across the pastel-tinted fields of fun in the sun.

Carl Marie von Weber's "Invitation to the Dance" receives an answer in our passage in 2 Samuel. Our dancing partner on this June day is not Arthur Murray in a ballroom, Fred Astaire in his top hat, or even Michael Jackson doing the most frantic break dance steps this side of Harlem.

Our dancer is David. David, the sweet psalm singer of Israel. David, whose name in Hebrew means "beloved" is seen before our eyes leaping like a lizard; shouting like a banshee and hollering like a University of Louisville fan in the final minutes of the Duke game.

A young girl was seen in front of a mail box jumping up and down like a jack rabbit and cheering with gusto. A bemused neighbor asked her what she was doing. "Simple," said the girls. "I'm trying out a few of the new cheers I just received in my cheerleading correspondence course."

Sometimes we need to take a course in joy. It seems as if joy has taken the slow boat to China and has left our home behind. We fear to smile except in Pepsodent commercials. or when we put on our Sunday finery for church. We have a streak of Puritanism in our Yankee souls. H. L. Mencken quipped that a Puritan was someone who feared that somewhere, someone was having a good time.

David was a happy warrior on that great day in the life of his nation and himself. The ark of the covenant containing the Ten Commandments was moved to Jerusalem by David and 30,000 of his followers. The most sacred of all objects in Israelite worship would be placed in a tent in the city of David.

Jerusalem would now become not only the political, but the religious, center of the nation. Here is how Joseph Heller, in his novel *God Knows*, imagines how David would describe that Joyous day of singing and rejoicing:

> *Where the ark was, there was God . . . you never heard so much music or saw so much rejoicing as there was on the day we brought the ark of the covenant up into the city . . . I was right out in front leading them all, dancing before the Lord . . . with all my might, clothed in a robe of fine linen . . .*"[1]

Most of us are dominated by the right sides of our brains — the side controlling hard thinking. There is nothing wrong with this. What is lamentable is when we don't allow the left side of our noggin to open the summertime of creativity calling us to praise the Lord with music and song and joy.

Hear how a jaded seminary professor rediscovered the joy of true worship:

> *God . . . I want . . .*
> *to surrender to the rhythm of music and sea*
> *to the seasons of ebb and flow,*
> *to the tidal surge of love*
>
> *I am tired of being*
> *hard,*
> *tight,*
> *controlled,*
> *tensed against the invasion of novelty,*
> *armed against tenderness,*
> *afraid of softness*

[1] Joseph Heller, *God Knows*, Alfred A. Knopf, New York, New York, 1984, pp. 262-263.

I am tired of
directing my world,

God give me madness
that does not destroy
wisdom
responsibility
love[2]

Nat King Cole sang, "Those lazy, hazy, crazy days of summer." Summer is a time for fun and travel. A time for family barbecues and trips to the golf course and the pool. Summer is a happy time. All of our activities this summer are to be enjoyed to the full. Yet in all of our vacationing joy, let us not forget that while fun is great, it can only serve as a dessert, and not the main course of life's banquet.

Let us find time to worship the Lord. Not in glum-faced, duty-bound obedience to some Puritan God, but in happy praise of him who is the Lord of all creaton.

[2] Sam Keen, *To A Dancing God, Harper Row, New York, New York, 1970, pp. 116-118.*

A Queen Bee's Sting   *2 Samuel 6:16-19*

The bee hive was abuzz. A human had stuck his hand into the hive and escaped with honey. Angry bees swarmed to God's court. They demanded that God grant them the power of stinging to death anyone who approached their honeycombs.

God was angry with the greedy bees who would not even share a Bit-o-Honey candy bar with their neighbors. Aesop, in his fable, tells us that God condemned the bees to instant death whenever they stung someone. The bees would be a chorus, adept at humming Paul's song about the sting of death.

Michal was a queen bee whose tongue was a sharp saber of stabbing insult. Gazing down from her window, she saw her husband David approaching the walls of Jerusalem. He was dancing with the joyful abandon of a Michael Jackson. His voice was vibrant with an Ode to Joy. Over thirty thousand of his people cheered the conquering hero home. David had defeated the Jebusites and made Jerusalem the capital of a united nation. He had brought the Ark, in which were stored the Ten Commandments, the ten miles from Kireath-jearim to its new home in the city of David. The Ark was the symbol of God. By bringing the saved Ark to Jerusalem, David was showing everyone that God and the nation of Israel were in charge in the land of Canaan. He was demonstrating to everyone that he was God's anointed. David, the giant killer, David, the psalm singer; David the Robin Hood-clad bandit, was now David the King. A bronze-faced monarch leading his merry men and women to glory.

Michal looked at this latest scene from her marriage with hatred brewing like a witch's stew in her heart.

Ingmar Bergman, the great Swedish director, scripted a movie called *Scenes from a Marriage*. In short scenes culled from the experience of a long marriage, we see the gradual disintegration of love between a husband and a wife. The writer of Samuel gives us short scenes from the marriage of David and Michal, two millenia before movies were invented. In the first scene we see Michal pursuing David with all the fanaticism of a Daisy Mae about to apprehend Lil Abner on the outskirts of Dogpatch.

Sibling rivalry had made her jealous of her big sister Merab, who loved David. The callow shepherd from Bethlehem melted when he saw Merab, but Saul forced her to marry someone else. Saul distrusted David and did not want to have him around as a son-in-law. Michal used all her feminine wiles on the old king. At last he told her she could marry David if the bridegroom to be would bring him the skins of 100 Philistines. David not only accomplished this martial feat, but brought in 200 Philistine foreskins!

David and Michal were married, but they hardly lived happily ever after. Saul was determined to kill David, whom he viewed as a rival for the throne. Michal caught wind of a plot to assassinate David and implored him to escape. Late one night assassins crawled up the stairway in the craggy palace at Gibeah and plunged a knife into David's heart. Or so they thought. Actually, the shrewd Michal had dressed up a dummy and covered it with a goats' hair blanket while David made a quick exit.

Years passed and Michal did not see David. Saul forced her into marriage with a man named Palti (Paltigh), and gradually she grew to love him, forgetting David. Suddenly her happiness was shattered forever. Jonathan and Saul were slain on Mount Gilboa and Abner, the general of Saul's armies, was forced to bring her to David in Hebron. Palti's uxorious heart was crushed by the steamroller fury of David's ire, as he snatched Michal from Palti's breast. Palti was a pathetic portrait of pain as he followed Michal to the outskirts of a village called Bahurim, nestled on the slopes of the Mount of Olives.

But Michal's royal heart was made of sterner stuff. Granite-faced she marched to her fate as a member of David's harem. Unlike the Mozart opera *The Abduction from the Seraglio*, this daughter of Saul knew her life would be spent in a silk-screened prison as just another of the courtesans forced to pay court to the king.

The last scene of the tragic wedlock of Michal and David was witnessed by the frenzied dancing of David. His orgiastic ecstasy was indecent and in disorder.

I can understand why Michal hated David. He had loved other women. He had been responsible for the death of many members of her family. He had been her father's greatest enemy. She had loved him as a girl, and had been scorned by him as a woman.

A woman once demanded that she receive a divorce because her husband washed her face each night. "Not granted!" snapped the judge. "After all, cleanliness is next to godliness." "That's not all he does!" she shouted. "After he washes my face, he irons it!"

Michal could not hope for a divorce. She was simply one of David's eight wives. She would be barren of children, and would have to put up with catty remarks for 1001 nights in the harem of a Middle Eastern sheik.

Why then does the author of Samuel seem to dislike Michal so much? Human motivations for hate or love or indifference are as tangled as the skein woven by fate. Perhaps the reason Michal is hated so much by Jewish tradition is because her hatred was not directed at David but at God. God had made David king and Michal could not accept this fact. God had moved the church she attended from Gibeah to a new location, and Michal could not accept the change. God had altered the *Book of Order* and the order of worship, and she could not stand the new hymns or the new way God was to be worshiped.

Some churches are so cold that the ushers have to wear ice skates. Some hearts are as hard as the pews we sit on on Sunday mornings. Some Christian craftsmen have plopped God into a box and tied him up with the ropes of reason. Some Christians buzz when a different-colored bee approaches the hive.

Michal had gripes against David, but she succumbed to what the psychologists call transference, blaming God for her troubles. She refused to realize that one sign of our trust in God is that we learn to roll with the punches of change. Change is frightening. Everything that is new does not glitter with gold. But change in worship and church life is as much a given as it is in every other human activity.

God grant that we will learn to flow with the tides of change. God grant that we will not be so tied to a building, or a preacher, or a denomination, or the old hymns that we will forget to worship him who makes old things new, him who gives us new life through the resurrection of David's Son, even Jesus the Christ.

A Dynasty of Destiny

2 Samuel 7:12-17

Proper 9 (July 3-9)

Dynasty and Dallas sit atop the slippery pole of the tube ratings. Catty Alexis and crafty J.R. pursue their juggernaut pace for the plums of power, prestige, and pelf.

In Los Angeles, fervid fans still hoot and holler for a Bruin roundball dynasty built by Goliaths of the goalpost named Jabbar and Walton. The Windsor dynasty is assured of a successor, as Prince William toddles along a London street under the watchful supervision of an attendant nanny. The Kennedy dynasty gathers in sorrow around the grave of a heroin victim. The Shah of Iran is deposed from power and a centuries-old dynasty crumbles under the scowling face of a bearded Ayatollah. Ours is an age of crumbling dynasties.

Dynasty comes from the Greek word *dynaste,* meaning power. It means the passing of power from father to son, from senior to freshman, from a retiring executive to his young assistant whom he has trained. A dynasty ensures that the torch of power will be passed along decently and in good order.

David had a rendezvous with destiny. He had followed the star of Bethlehem from the sheepfields to the splendors of a newly built cedar palace. He was rich and famous. He was a Godfather more feared than Al Capone. He was a religious leader venerated with the same gusto as Americans express in admiration of a Billy Graham. He was an administrator and organizer of a loose band of tribes into a united nation called Israel.

Sitting alone one night, David wondered what would happen to his empire when he went the way of all flesh. He longed to be assured that the worship of God and rule by one of his sons would continue. He called for Nathan the prophet. We know little about Nathan, but we do know that he was honest and stern, and his character bears a close similarity to that prophetic giant Samuel.

Nathan told David that while he would not be permitted to build God a temple, it would be built by his son. He also told him that David's descendants would always reign in the kingdom.

We are not sure when the Deuteronomic historian wrote this tale of David and Nathan. It may well have been in the black days of the exile. It may have been written at a time when mighty Israel had fallen under the jackbooted terror of the Babylonian blitzkrieg.

Why, then, did this story win popularity among a people beaten black and blue? After all, David's sons had ended up between a rock and a hard place. David's kingdom had disappeared under the sands of a desert resounding to the beat of Babylonian hoofbeats. It was as if magician David Copperfield were not making cards disappear, but was ordering that hope fade like an old pair of designer jeans.

An everlasting kingdom for David's house? A kingdom of peace and prosperity and joy? Laughable. Absurd. Pipedreams for pied pipers leading nowhere.

Yet the editor's stylus wrote the words about the everlasting kingdom. The people heard and read and believed. Hope was born in their hearts that someday, in some way, the kingdom of David would live again, incarnated in a Son of David who would set his people free.

The centuries beat against the shore of time. At last, on a black and still night in the house of bread called "Bethlehem," a Son of David was born. He never owned a house, and had not even been born in a house. He was a carpenter who built a house for everyone. He once angrily cried out that his house was to be a house of prayer for all people. The door to his house is always open to welcome his children. The windows of his house let in the strong breeze of Holy Spirit which blows where it will, as it stirs winds of justice and mercy in the hearts of men. The kitchen table is always set with the bread of his body and the blood of his sacrifice.

In a church office I saw a painting by a French painter whose name I have forgotten. It shows the Son of David entering a humble peasant home located in the French countryside. The grey-haired mother of a large family is setting the table for dinner. Her husband, tired from a day in the fields, gathers with their children at the door as their guest for the evening enters. Today their guest is standing at our doors. John Wesley, when refused admittance to the churches of his day, preached in the open fields, saying, "My parish is the world."

The Son of David's parish is the world. He is a Son who shall never experience an eclipse. He is a friend who sticks closer than a brother. He is a father who dies for his children on a cross.

Come home to him today and claim your dynatic birthright as a child of God. He has given you the gift of eternal life in a kingdom whose glory shall never be tarnished, and whose promise gives us hope for the future. Sing with James Montgomery as we hail in faith great David's greater Son, Jesus the Christ:

> *The time of time shall never*
> *His covenant remove;*
> *His Name shall stand forever;*
> *That Name to us is Love. Amen*

Promising Words
2 Samuel 7:18-29
Proper 10 (July 10-16)

A photo album is a magic carpet ride into the realm of memory. Like leaves of October tinted with the auburn and golden hues of autumn, snapshots are colored with the rich pastels of previous events. *Saturday Review* editor Norman Cousins has written of his feelings about snapshots in his book, *Human Options,*

> *A man (woman) comes to know himself through the pictures he takes ... in ... reviewing the hundreds of pictures I have taken ... in many parts of the world ... I learn ... the camera is more than a box that records an external situation ... it is also turned inwards.*[1]

David had a visual mind. As a shepherd he was alert to the changing seasons affecting the sheep he cared for with love. His eyes saw the green pastures and the dark valleys. As a warrior he had learned to observe the "lay of the land" behind which enemies might lurk. As a poet his art was enriched by the colorful ceremonies in which he took part at the festive seasons of the Hebrew liturgical year. David had stored such visual memories in his mind to *remember*, and they would *refresh* him in weary moments. Now David had seen his fondest dreams become reality. Kingship of a people in his grasp, he had now been called from the fields of Bethlehem to lead the children of Israel.

In the gloaming of a quiet evening, the author of 2 Samuel limns a portrait of King David at prayer. We see the shepherd king as he bows in silence before the ark of the covenant. David has wisely moved this potent symbol with his people of God's presence from its shrine in Shiloh to Jerusalem. The ark is now located in the center of Israel. David reflects and recalls his past battles; his present triumphs and the future

---

[1] Norman Cousins, *Human Options,* pp. 128-129, Berkley Books, New York, New York, 1981.

hopes he has for his people as he prays before the Lord God.

In one of the great prayers in the Old Testament, David remembers the scenes of God's shepherding care for his pilgrim people. The God who guided his flock through the stormy waters of captivity in Egypt is he who is the Lord of Liberation. David's soul vaults like a hart leaping over a purling stream, as he rehearses in his mind's eye scenes of God's mighty acts in the arena of a nation's sacred memory.

The God he worships is a Lord of three tenses — past, present, and future. As Ruth Thomas expresses in her poem, "The Untried Way":

> The same Yesterday — the God behind me, the God of the
> ages
> The same Today, the God beside me, with His guiding hand
> The same Forever — the God before me in the dim, unknown
> future.[2]

David turns the page of his scrapbook memory and discovers scenes in which a shepherd boy defeated a Philistine Giant. Other photos in his memory bank portray that Robin Hood glen, where he recruited doughty mighty men eager and willing to fight for a nation's freedom against godless foes. Tender moments are captured in snapshots of a lamb helped by a shepherd boy eager to remove a thorn from soft flesh. Memories of home are stirred as the king sees the faces of Jesse and his brothers. Flashcubes pop as David recalls the shepherd God who has never deserted him on his rise to power.

As David prays in the Tent of the Ark of the Covenant, I too remember the path I have traveled in my cursory study of this man of God. I recall that,

> David had risen to lead a flock when there was no king in
> sight;
> Bowed to sing a psalm to scatter the clouds of his soul's
> dark night;

[2] Herbert Lockyear, God's Book of Poetry, Thomas Nelson Co., Nashville, 1983, poem quoted on page 171 by Ruth Thomas.

Danced before God with abandon as the ark of the covenant
came to Jerusalem spreading God's holy light
Prayed to the God of love for guidance to shepherd Israel
with holy justice and might.[3]

As a Civil War buff, I have often pored over the pages of Bruce Catton's *A Stillness at Appamatox*. As I gaze into the stilled tent where David prays, I see a great king adoring the King of kings and Lord of lords. "A Stillness in Jerusalem," as deep as the night shining with the fire of a heart aflame with love of the Creator God, burns with fury throughout the fresco of time.

David's mood of praise at this moment is well captured in the great Psalm 18:

I love thee, O Lord, my strength
The Lord is my rock and my fortress and my deliverer
my God, my rock, in whom I take refuge,
my shield, and the horn of my salvation, my stronghold
... to my God I cried for help ... he heard my voice
and my cry to him reached his ears.

David is not only a worshiper of a God of the past. His God is a Lord of the future, guiding his children into the adventure of tomorrow. David teaches us to trust the Lord who has guided us this far, and who will be with us until our journey has reached a safe harbor. Theologian Helmut Thielicke expresses his trust in God's future care when he writes, "It is true that I do not know what is coming, but I know who is coming. Therefore, I can drain the moment in which I live, laughing and weeping ... with the face of God shining on me ... we can catch a fleeting glimpse of the magnitude of the future by the down payment we have already received."[4]

David's God was not confined to a musty album of faded and tattered snapshots. His God was the pioneer of faith who guides us into his kingdom. May God grant us the courage and loyalty needed to follow our pilgrim God with strength and fortitude.

[3] Poem by Michael Mills, 1987.
[4] Helmut Thielicke, *I Believe, I Believe*, Fortress Press, Philadelphia, 1968, p. 214.

A Father's Friend   *2 Samuel 9:1-6*

The phone buzzed with the fury of a bumblebee chomping into a Bit-o-Honey candy bar. A baritone voice reminiscent of Sherill Milnes' dulcet tones purrs into the receiver, "Good morning, I am a computer."

In this chapter we honor a man, not a Rube Goldberg crafted machine. *Time* magazine recently presented a resume on a sampling of commencement speeches given to our graduating seniors. A theme common in many of these speeches is about the dangers we face in a big, impersonal society which treats people as things and things as people.

George Orwell's Big Brother relished treating people as numbers whose names were not important. Sometimes we treat Dad as if he were a machine; a machine we crank and dollar bills fall into our hands with the ease of a bank money machine user; a machine that helps keep the machine we drive in running order; a robot we expect to wear many different hats. A Little League baseball cap for his coaching duties. A khaki-colored hat for Boy Scout advisor duty, and an old hat to keep the sun off as he toils in mom's garden behind the garage.

Back in the 1890's, tragedy had sounded a death knell to a family in Big Bend River, near Spokane, Washington. William Jackson Smart had just buried his wife. She had left him with five small boys and a baby girl to raise.

In the spring of 1910 the girl, now an adult, was attending a Mother's Day service at church. She thought to herself, "My Dad was the only mother I knew." The idea of Father's Day was born that day in the heart of Mrs. John Dodd. Inspired by Mrs. Dodd, we echo William Wordsworth's words in his Ecclesiastical Sonnets, "Father — to God himself we cannot give a holier name."

A father is not a machine. He is not questing with quixotic intensity for the soul of a new machine. A father is a man, and like a man, is prey, as we all are, to the agonies as well as the ecstasies of life.

Our role is to make our fathers proud of us. Martin Luther once plucked a rose from his garden and said that, if a man could make such a flower, he would be thought great. Fathers give life to children who are to bloom with a goodness reflecting the character of their Fathers.

Our story today deals with a son who was a wilting rose. A mediocre son of a great man. His name was Mephibosheth. Like Tiny Tim, he was crippled. But his father had been the mighty warrior Jonathan. On the day his father was slain by the Philistines on the bloody slopes of Mount Gilboa, Mephibosheth had become crippled. His panicky nurse had dropped him as she ran through the palace.

Mephibosheth was sent away to a tiny hamlet called LoDebar, meaning "of no account," to be raised by a peasant named Machir. As one of the few survivors of Saul's family, it was felt that David, Saul's greatest enemy would kill Mephibosheth if he caught the lad.

Years passed, and one day a servant of Saul's told David that Mephibosheth still lived. Then David proved what a good and loyal friend he was, for had remained faithful to his covenant of loving brotherhood with Jonathan. In fairy tale fashion he ordered Ziba to bring Mephibosheth to his palace. He ordered Ziba to provide Mephibosheth with an estate and see that he would always be given a place at David's table.

Mephibosheth was called from his welfare shack in a Galilean backwater to the halls of jet-set splendor in Jerusalem. David waved his magic wand of power and all ended well for the son of his best friend.

Think of the rich symbolism of this tale, which might have been lifted from the pages of the *Arabian Nights.* Mephibosheth lived in a town called "nowhere," in the home of a man named Machir, whose name in Hebrew means "sold." The Son of David called Mephibosheth to his royal banquet table groaning with rich meats and heavy with delicious cheeses.

Like Mephibosheth, we too are lamed. Lamed not by a nurse's hasty fall, but by sin. Like him we are exiled from God's love until the Son of David cries for us to return to his flock. From Calvary's cross Jesus urges us to return to his table. From the Garden's empty tomb he bids us to rise into new life. From the table of the Upper Room he invites us to eat and drink in his company.

God is a Father whose door is always open to welcome his prodigal sons and daughters home. We can all rejoice that God loves us with a father's love. We rejoice in Saint Augustine's assurance that God loves each of us as if there were no one else in all the universe to love. We rejoice too that God is our Father, Christ is our brother, and the Holy Spirit is our guide. We thank God for his fatherly care. With F. W. Faber we sing:

Faith of our fathers! living still
In spite of dungeon, fire and sword
O how our hearts beat high with joy
Whene'er we hear that glorious word
Faith of our Fathers, holy faith!
We will be true to thee, till death. Amen[1]

[1] "Faith of Our Fathers," from *Worship Book of the Presbyterian Church,* Westminster Press, Philadelphia, 1973.

The Singer and the Siren 2 Samuel 11:2-5, 26-27

Proper 11 (July 17-23)

I would rather not mention it. Centuries of rabbis have spilt gallons of ink thinking up excuses for him. The author of Chronicles doesn't waste a jot or tittle in telling the tale. After all, who enjoys slicing another hefty chink in a hero's armor?

Lord Protector Oliver Cromwell told Sir Peter Lely to paint his portrait with the warts and all. Yet I have trouble brush-stroking out the black deeds of David.

Shortly after he had been convicted for throwing the 1919 World Series, the great outfielder Shoeless Joe Jackson was accosted by a small tyke who pleaded, "Say it ain't so, Joe, say it ain't so." The sordid tale of David and Bathsheba is so. No amount of DeHart Deluxe Latex will wipe away their sin. Michelangelo's statue of David portrays him as if he were about to line up for the hundred yard dash at the Olympics. Nary a worry wart line scampers in wild abandon across David's forehead.

Encountering David on a sultry Jerusalem afternoon, we see deep lines etched into his forehead. Lines scratched with the steel stylus of sin. Commandments were about to be broken. Promises were about to be crushed in the winepress of passion. For the kingly eye roving like a fox stalking a yearling lamb had spied a tempting treat. Bathsheba, whose name means "Daughter of the Sabbath" was bathing in the evening glow of a candle. David peered down from his rooftop and saw Bathsheba soaping herself with olive oil and the residue of burnt plants. Because like Lola in *Damn Yankees*, David's song is "Whatever Lola wants, Lola gets," the scenario of greed and adultery and murder was staged for all of us to see.

Contemporaneous with David's tenth century B.C. reign was the Greek ruler of Ithaca, named Odysseus (called Ulysses by the Romans). Homer says that when Odysseus was sailing back to Greece after the Trojan war was ended, his ship passed stony rocks near Sicily. Here were sitting several sirens who were half-bird and half-woman. Their hobby was to lure sailors and their ships to destruction by their singing. But Odysseus foiled their plans. He stuffed the ears of his crewmen with wax and had them tie him to the mast, so that the sirens could not woo him to his doom. David had no wax and no rope available. His lust was as unbridled as a three-year-old rounding the clubhouse turn on Derby Day at Churchhill Downs.

Biblical scholars know little about Bathsheba, the bathing beauty who became David's mistress and wife. It is known, however, that she was married to Uriah, a Hittite warrior. Uriah was away from Jerusalem fighting before the gates of Rabbah, which is now Amman, Jordan. Bathsheba's father and grandfather were trusted advisors of the king. Bathsheba was an aristocratic young lady and a legendary beauty.

David had a torrid affair with Bathsheba, who learned to her dismay, that she was heavy with child. Deceitful David was no longer the guileless shepherd lad. He became a cowardly lion fearful of the discovery of his adultery. With malice in his heart, and murder in his hastily sketched blueprint of brutality, he lured Uriah home with an order. David reasoned that Uriah would have sex with Bathsheba and the populace would reason that it was Uriah who had fathered the unborn child.

David then ordered Uriah to carry a message to Joab, his commanding general. The note which the obedient Uriah brought to Joab was, unbeknownst to Uriah, his own death warrant. The note was an order from David to Joab to put Uriah in the forefront of the battle, so he would be killed. The plan worked. Uriah was killed. David had his Bathsheba. The foul murder plot against Uriah is reminiscent of that hatched by the lovers in James M. Cain's novel *The Postman Always Rings Twice*. In Cain's novel, the guilty lovers kill the husband and then betray each other as they are tortured by the guilt of their foul deed.

It is not known if Bathsheba plotted with David in his Cain-like slaying of her husband. It is known, however, that the child of Bathsheba and David became ill and died.

God was greatly displeased at what David had done. He had committed adultery. He had sent an innocent man to his death. Like any ancient oriental satrap, he had worshiped power, and what power can do, in order to get what he wanted.

What does this sordid tale mean to us? One thing it means to me is that the Bible is unflinching in its honesty. Even the great men and women of the Bible are portrayed with all their flaws, all their warts, and all their sins clearly showing.

Like David, you and I have seen something in life's candy store and grabbed for it. Power politics is a game played not only by congressmen types in Washington. Wanting what we want so badly that we will let nothing stand in the way of our getting it is a temptation we face each day, in the kitchen with the girls playing Bunko, at the bowling alley with the boys, and at the workbench, or over the water cooler at the office. In whatever form of power politics we are playing, let us not forget what David so blithely disregarded. He forgot that the postman rings twice. The death of Uriah was balanced with the death of the child. Truth breaking leads to grave consequences.

The Reverend Maltbie Babcock was on target when he sang that this is "My Father's World." God is running an orderly and decent universe. When we break his laws we will be punished. The good news is that though God is our great judge, he is also our Father. Jesus Christ has come to us so that we might be forgiven of our sins and restored to fellowship with God. In our pride and our passion, in our denials of God and worship of self, let us cling to the old rugged cross where in the broken body of Christ we shall find our forgiveness.

David's psalm of repentance is played anew on the human heart's harp of hope each time we ask and receive the Lord's forgiveness:

Have mercy on me, O God,
according to thy steadfast love . . .
Create in me a clean heart, O God
and take not thy holy spirit from me.
Restore to me the joy of thy salvation
and uphold me with a willing spirit. Amen
                                    (Psalm 51:12; 10-12)

A Ewe Turn

2 Samuel 12:1-7
Proper 12 (July 24-30)

He made an abrupt U-turn on Easy Street. His applecart of greed was overturned. Max Factor makeup could not mask the portrait of guilt sketched on his face. His gut growled with the gruff voice of self-loathing. Shame squeezed his body with the smothering grip of a boa constrictor. Portrait of a robber baron. Portrait of a bad shepherd whose blackest sheep was his own soul. Portrait of a thief who had discovered his own hand caught in the cookie jar.

His Rip Van Winkle soul had been awakened by the still small voice of Nathan. Nathan had long been a faithful servant of David. Nathan was also a faithful disciple of God. Nathan knew that God's covenant of love with David had been broken. David had murdered his lieutenant Uriah so he could have the soldier's wife Bathsheba for his own. Bathsheba, with whom he had already committed adultery. Bathsheba, already carrying David's child. A child that would not live.

Nathan was a brave spokesman for truth. His name in Hebrew means "God has given." God had given Nathan many gifts. He had already helped David arrange musical worship in the sanctuary. (2 Chronicles 29:25) Earlier Nathan fired straight from the hip, telling David that, because of his bloody hands, he was not to build the Temple.

Nathan again stood before his master's throne. Again Nathan's face is a profile of courageous defiance of his earthly lord. Nathan faced a difficult task. His assignment was to obliquely lead David to a realization of the sorrow which his sin with Bathsheba had brought to the heart of God. Nathan, who like Sancho Panza, had a facility for spinning parables, told one of the greatest of all parables uttered in the Bible. It is his peerless parable of the little ewe lamb. A parable so poignant, powerful, and pertinent to his own *Sitz im Leben* that it brought David to his knees in humble repentance before God's throne.

Pet lambs were popular in ancient Israel. Nathan knew that a story about a ewe would be appealing to David's shepherds. Nathan told of a poor man who had a pet lamb. He had bought it with hard earned money. He had loved it so much that the little lamb was allowed to eat at the family table and even sleep in the family sleeping chamber.

There was a rich man. He had so many sheep that they looked like marshmallows as they frolicked across the sun-kissed fields of spring.

The rich man was a covetous rogue. One day a wayfarer stopped by to visit him. The prince decided to rob the pauper. He pilfered the ewe lamb and turned the wooly creature into lambchops for his guest.

David's heart growled with silent revulsion at the wickedness of the rich man of the parable. Nathan's withered voice, cracked with age, was proving to be a power drill, driving deep into David's tortured and guilt-blanketed psyche. David ordered the rich man to be executed for his cruelty. Unvoiced but insistent, his tell-tale heart beat out the drumbeat of self-revulsion as he remembered his own robbery. His own theft of Bathsheba from Uriah's bosom was a metastasizing cancer. Time was powerless to whitewash the greasepaint of adulterous greed.

Then in one of the great accusations in all world literature, Nathan pointed his finger at the king and roared, "You are the man!" Uriah had a little lamb whose name was Bathsheba. David, not content with a full harem of wives, wanted Bathsheba. To win her he had not stopped at adultery or murder. What Sigmund Freud called the "id" of unbridled passion had conquered David's super-ego of moral obedience to God.

David awoke with a hangover of heartache at what he had done. At last, he saw himself as the big bad wolf who had preyed on the sheepfold. At last, he could face his sin and deal with it. At last, he could walk back to the courts of his Creator.

David learned the hard way that God is a Lord of loving forgiveness. He also learned that even when we are forgiven, we often are forced to live with the consequences of our sins. No amount of confession would resurrect the slain Uriah from his grave. The adultery with Bathsheba could not be easily erased, as she was heavy with child. David emerged from these sordid chapters of his life's journal a wiser and sadder man.

David is everyman. Unlike Nathan, I have trouble pointing my finger at David. Americans are the rich pinnacle perched atop a pyramid of poverty. We live in a consumer society which equates more with better. Every day the sirens of the media whisper in our ears to buy now and pay later. We have much, but the Jones' next door have a new car. We trust Master Card instead of the Master, as we sail away on another shopping spree. We are rich Babylon in love with the bangles, baubles, and beads of an industrialized society.

In his long story of the Soviet Union's concentration camps, *The Gulag Archipelago*, Aleksandr I. Solzhenitsyn, the 1970 Nobel Laureate in Literature, tells a heartwarming tale. In 1929 whole masses of peasants were forcibly moved to Siberia. One of these peasants was named Timofey. One day tax collectors came and seized all of the family's furniture. They soon returned and grabbed all the sticks of furniture in the hovel. At last, they came and took the three little ewe lambs which Timofey's children loved as pets. The children had hid their wooly friends, but the ruthless power of the government discovered and stole them.[1]

Once there was a teacher who owned nothing, a rabbi who told a rich young ruler to give his gold away and follow him.

---

[1] Aleksandr I. Solzhenitsyn, *The Gulag Archipelago*. Volume 3, pp. 357-359, Harper & Row Co., New York, 1979.

He was known as the Son of David. He came so that the rich
might repent and enter into the rich kingdom of love. A kingdom whose doors are open to the poor and despised. A kingdom ruled by him who was taken like a ewe lamb and slain
so that the rich of his day could feast on his broken bones.

He is the good shepherd who loves the bad shepherds,
and those in their flock whom they have injured. His name
is Jesus, and he is calling us in this hour to repent of our sins.
He is calling us to feed the hungry, clothe the naked, and help
the helpless. How shall we answer him?

Death Watch   *2 Samuel 12:15-24*

Proper 13 (July 31-August 8)

The angel of death seized the ripe apple of David's eye. The sounds of wailing assaulted his ear. The icy brow of his child sent shivers of grief cascading down his bowed back. Death had not visited Pharaoh's first born way down in Egypt land. Death had defeated for a season the caliph of courage called David. David knew where death's sting was. Its sharp needle had penetrated the citadel of his broken heart.

David held the body of his boy to his bosom. The child had been born out of wedlock. His broken body symbolized David's broken faith with God.

For seven days as the moribund child lay ill, the great king cried out to God for the lad's recovery. He cast off the purple of office for the sackcloth and ashes of a penitence. David's ruddy face was covered with the grime of lying on the dusty earth in humble despair.

Whispering hopelessness was swept to the king's ears on the fleet-winged words of his counselors. "Would the king kill himself if his boy died? Who would take over the reigns of the kingdom if David trod into the valley of death?" "Would the king become insane and perhaps inaugurate a slaughter of the innocents?"

Such questions buzzed throughout the beehive of the royal court. At last the good physicians came to the sorrowing father with the bad news. No miracle heart transplant was available for this baby. No answer to prayer for the child's life. God had taken the baby and David was left to mourn.

David was a sinner and his sin with Bathsheba was punished. Most men would have been crushed by the infant's death. God is not a cruel God who slaughters babies. The baby simply died in an age of high infant mortality, when disease was as common as the steamy desert sirocco of sand stirring in the tents of the shepherds.

Yet the consequence of David's sin was the birth of the babe. David had to live with the death of his child. Nothing would bring his son back.

What would David do? He dressed in his purple; shaved and went to the House of the Lord. He got on with his life. In the depths of grief, David forced words of praise to issue from his mouth. No wonder it has been said of this shepherd-king, "For one fleeting moment a star crossed the firmament of Israel illuminating the uppermost heights and profoundest depths of human existence."[1]

David knew how to cope with grief. He was able to express his hurt and his honest hostility. He faced the fact that his son's face would no longer light up his day. King David knew too that he must go on living, learning, and worshiping the living God. He hoped for a reunion with his son, but he did not love and worship God because of his certainty of belief in immortal life. David loved the Lord because He had never forsaken him in moments of sin and in seasons of sorrow. God was the Covenant Lord whose "hesed," or loving mercy was never AWOL from hurting people.

All of us face the death of people we love. We can deny our hurt by covering our grief with silver clouds of piety. Or we can pour out our anguish and doubt to a God who is there in the pit of pain with us. A God who also has lost a firstborn son. A God whose son died upon a cross of shame.

David's cry, "Is the child dead?" is answered for us in the word of the man at the tomb, "He is Risen!" Because He lives, we live too and those we love await us at Heaven's Gate. The words of John Donne yet ring true:

[1] Henry Biberfeld, *David King of Israel*, Feldheim Co., Jerusalem, 1978, p. 79.

I have a sin of fear, that when I have spun
My last thread
I shall perish on the shore;
But swear by Thyself that at my death
Thy Son
Shall shine as he shines now . . .
I fear no more.

A Princely Passion   *2 Samuel 13:1-5, 15-19*

She has just passed her twenty-fifth birthday. A pert miss, young, attractive, and popular. Possessing more threads in her closet than could be found on your Singer Sewing Machine's spool. She is a doll. She is rich and famous. Her name is Barbie.

Her boyfriend is tall, dark, and handsome. His tennis outfit would make Jimmy Connors' eyes turn green with envy. His tailor-made gloves would make the likes of Michael Jackson drool with jealousy. His well-tailored suits are a model for budding executives on Broadway. He is Ken. Like Barbie, he, too, is a doll.

Ken and Barbie are not real. They do not spring into action when the department store closes for the night and the mannequins make merry.

Once upon a time, there were two dolls. In this chapter we look at their story, which begins in fairy tale enchantment and ends in nightmarish tragedy.

She walked like an angel and talked like an angel. Her name was Tamar, meaning in Hebrew "a Palm." She was a gentle breeze blowing across a hot desert. Her eyes were deep pools of refreshment. Her loveliness was an oasis in a desert landscape. She was a princess without a prince charming.

He was a prince, but he was far from charming. Amnon was more in the mode of a Machiavellian Prince. Machiavelli, who had written that a prince "... must be a fox to recognize traps and a lion to frighten wolves."[1]

Amnon's problem was Amnon. He worshiped himself and his desires to the exclusion of all else. Like a cat in a canary cage, he was king of the hill. The eldest son of David

[1] Niccolo Machiavelli, *The Prince*, New American Library, New York, 1964, p. 92.

and heir to the throne. Well-helled and well-fed. Allowed to ride on one of the specially groomed royal donkeys, which today would be comparable to a sleek Ferrari.

Amnon was the son of King David. David was a child of a depressed economy. An economy bereft of the talents of a David Stockman or the defense capabilitities of the joint chiefs of staff in conclave at the Pentagon. David had seen hunger, defeat, and death as he grew to manhood in the days of his youth. David had come to maturity in an Israel relying on slingshot strength to subdue the iron spears of Philistine power.

David, who had come from rags to riches, poured those riches on Amnon's head. Amnon was, after all, David's first-born son. A son of David who had first seen light in his fugitive father's Hebron hideaway. A son of David who had seen the Lion of Judah claw his way to what Disraeli was wont to call the "top of the slippery pole" of political power.

Graduates of a small Oklahoman town high school in a Steinbeckesque dust bowl spring of 1934 talked on television with Bill Moyers. They told Bill that the trouble with the class of 1984 is that they are spoiled. Some even confessed to Moyers that they are responsible for the spoilation process. "We didn't have much so we gave our kids too much."

Amnon was the apple of David's eye. But he was also the bad apple in the barrel.

In the *Damn Yankees* musical, the seductive songstress sings, "Whatever Lola wants, Lola gets." That tune could have been Amnon's theme song. He saw his half-sister Tamar and he wanted her. With the assistance of a scheming relative he devised a plan to lure the lady into his spider's web. He pretended to be sick, so she would bring him one of her heart-shaped boiled cakes. Then he would spring on her, even as the wolf trapped Little Red Riding Hood. The ploy worked and Tamar was forced to yield to her wicked half-brother. His prize was won, but it left an unpleasant taste in his mouth. He loathed Tamar because he loathed himself. He refused to make her an honest woman by marrying her. He could have done this since, in Hebrew society, a half-brother could wed his half-sister. Even Father Abraham had married his half-sister Sarah. He could have confessed his foul deed to David, who was no moral paragon himself, as we have already seen in the sordid Bathsheba tale.

Amnon did none of these things. What he did do was kick the disgraced Tamar out of his private palace with the violence of Pat Summerall kicking a pigskin through the uprights. The disgraced princess was forced to take refuge with her brother Absalom.

David revealed his parental pusillanimity by refusing to discipline the undisciplined rapist Amnon. Amnon sulked in his playboy mansion, while Tamar wailed her song of betrayed innocence into the receptive ears of revenge-minded Absalom.

It is hard for us to find simple moralism in this tale. At least it does show that the Bible is honest in reporting on human sin. David and his family in no way resemble lily white gods to be worshiped. It shows, too, what happens when parents spoil their children. David gave Amnon everything but himself. The Lion of Judah was too busy fighting, feuding, and lusting to have much time to devote to Amnon. Like many a busy suburbanite mom or dad, he had time for everyone and everything, but no time for his family.

Centuries rolled by with the inevitable ebb and tide of events washing over humanity's shore. In an obscure village another Son of David was born. In a town known as Bethlehem of Judea. He had nothing from his parents but the gift of love. His palace was an open sky on a path from Galilee to Golgotha. His passion was for people. He was a Prince of Peace and not a Prince of Power.

He was raped by a rapacious rabble, clamoring for his blood. Like Tamar, he experienced shame and degradation.

He too knew the "ice water down the back" feeling of rejection. His name is Jesus. He is the Son of David, and today is the ruler of a Kingdom of Love.

Today, he hangs from a cross as he sees a young girl raped on Market Street. Tonight, he goes to bed hungry with the starving in Delhi and Detroit. Tomorrow, he will go to the unemployment office with the widow in Wichita. Next week, he will attend the funeral of the Iranian soldier and the Guatemalan peasant struck down by hit squads. He is the suffering shepherd who bleeds for his people.

He is the King of kings and Lord of lords. He is Son of David and Son of God. He is Jesus the Christ.

Getting Even   *2 Samuel 13:20-23, 28-29*

All men are not created equal. Neither are all women. A trip around the block teaches us that there are people with more talent, brains, bucks, and luck than we. Carl Lewis races for the gold on Pegasus-winged feet, while we huff and puff around the block. Our best friend arrives at the high school reunion in a Mercedes and boasts of his home in the Bahamas. Our son is a whiz on the Wang Computer, while we still have trouble balancing the check book.

Life is as unfair as ten rounds between ourselves and Muhammad Ali. Sometimes it seems that the rich do get richer and the poor get poorer. Sometimes it seems as if Mr. Lucky will never knock on our door. Because life is often unfair, some of us rail against the "slings and arrows of outrageous fortune." We become vigilantes who take the law into our own hands. Captains of our egotistical souls, bent on guiding our ships to some cozy harbor of power and security.

In 1973 Richard Nixon became our only President to resign the Executive Office. Shortly before his helicopter lifted off from the White House lawn, Nixon told reporters, "Those who hate you don't win, unless you hate them, and then you destroy yourself."[1]

When the obnoxious guy at the next desk gets the promotion. When our curvaceous neighbor brags about her success at Weight Watchers, while we sadly bite down another tuna fish sandwich in an effort to lose a pound. When we discover that Leo Durocher's remark about nice guys finishing last seems to be true in our case, then we taste the dregs of despair.

Lord Byron wrote that "sweet is revenge." We plot and plan and pour ice water into our veins, as cold-bloodedly we prepare to defeat the peacock proud "Mr. Goodbar" who boasts about his "goodies."

[1] Richard Nixon, *Time,* August 13, 1984.

Since life is unfair, our goal becomes getting even by any means possible. Most of us have had some experience when we have wanted someone to take a Humpty-Dumpty tumble off the wall. Times when we have covertly longed for some bad egg to crack. Dreams have flitted across our soul's landscape in which we have finally beaten the Joneses next door. Such thoughts are natural and we have all had them. Maturity gives us the courage to bridle those wild stallions, envy, jealousy, and revenge. Christian faith gives us time to pause and reflect upon our own blessings, talents, and opportunities.

Revenge of the Body Snatchers is much more than a science fiction flick. It is descriptive of those who would like to harm someone else in an effort to get even with them. A revengeful person seeks to transform somebody else into a nobody. He or she seeks to exact an eye for an eye and a tooth for a tooth.

Revengeful people and nations bear an unseemly affinity with Peter Pan. Like Sir James Barrie's eternal adolescent, revengeful people never grow up. They refuse to forgive and forget. They refuse to turn the other cheek and go the extra mile.

Absalom was a victim of the Peter Pan syndrome. He refused to grow up. Because Amnon had raped his sister, he decided to take justice into his own strong hands. Ice water flowed in his veins as he plotted the murder of his half-brother Amnon. With Florence Nightingale care he nursed his vengeance. His face was as silent as a Detroit factory before the arrival of the first shift. His demeanor was as placid as an Indiana farm lake in the hushed stillness of a springtime dawn. Yet underneath the surface, Absalom's soul seethed in a cauldron of murderous hatred. He cunningly invited his father to attend a sheep-shearing festivity at his farm near Baal Hazor. David refused, as business matters pressed heavily on his weary brow. Amnon took his father's place. Sheep-shearing among the ancient Hebrews was much like a harvest festival, but it was also a religious celebration.

Absalom had plotted to do away with Amnon at the festival. At his behest, his servants stabbed the rapist when he was deep in his cups of Mogen David. Amnon fell to the knives of his assassins, while the rest of David's sons fled from the bloody feast. They reasoned that, if Absalom had struck Amnon down, then perhaps they might be next. Absalom wanted no rivals for the throne and nothing would stop his juggernaut drive to power.

Absalom's later life would prove that he who lives by the sword dies by the sword. He had forgotten that revenge is a scimitar sharp two-edged blade. It cuts our enemy down, but like a boomerang it brings us down as well.

The sons of David. Amnon a rapist and a roustabout. Absalom more complex in nature. A strong silent John Wayne type. A patriot. A force to be reckoned with. Yet ultimately Absalom was guilty of the foul crime of murder. He became a Cain slaying his brother Abel.

Long after the days of Absalom and Amnon there was born another Son of David. Like Amnon he too was murdered at a sheep-shearing festival in which he was the sacrificial lamb. He came with words of forgiveness and not revenge. He came to bind us together with the ties of brotherhood, not to divide us with the weapons of revenge.

He is the Son of David and the Son of God. He is the Lamb who takes away the sins of the world. He is the suffering servant who is rejected and reviled among men.

Christ calls a world sundered into scowling camps of nuclear hostility to gaze upwards toward the suffering servant silhouetted against Golgotha's brooding hill. Jesus of Nazareth pleads with Moscow and Washington, and the homes where we hang our own shingles, to embrace the biblical concept of Shalom. Shaloma, definitive of peace and brotherhood and love. Shalom, described with prophetic insight captured in stirring metaphor by Micah of old:

> ... they shall beat their swords into plowshares and their spears into pruning hooks; nation shall not lift up sword against nations, neither shall they learn war any more; but they shall sit every man under his vine and under his fig tree and none shall make them afraid.
>
> *(Micah 4:3-4)*

In our own lives we can make a start on the journey to the Kingdom of God. We can pledge ourselves to lives of humble service. We can throw the golden crown of revenge down before the cross of Christ, in which we put our trust.

The Prodigal Prince   *2 Samuel 14:1-11*

Whispering unheeded advice to a Bloomington-bound scholar boarding a Greyhound. Masking a stray tear with mascara as your princess parades down the aisle to Mendelssohn and her prince. Waving farewell to your favorite recruit as he stands among the gaggle of GIs clustered in the chill predawn light of an airport runway. AT&T words flying with magic carpet speed as you urge your San Francisco-based son to eat more, spend less, and get to bed on time. You long for a glimpse of your daughter's baby boy; but know you can't afford the airfare to Atlanta.

Miles may separate parents from a child, but the umbilical cord of love is rarely torn asunder. One of the tragedies of life occurs when parents and children are separated not merely by school or job responsibilities. Instead, angry words and rash deeds can sever the tie that binds parents and children.

We have all disagreed and quarreled with our parents. If we are parents we have not always agreed that curfew time should be at 3 A.M., or that it would be such a good idea to drop out of school. Disagreements are natural in every parent-child relationship. Teenage rebellion against parents is a part of growing up. The problem comes when both parents and children are adults and have come to distrust and, at times, even hate each other.

Roberta Flack has a lyric which goes, "the first time ever I saw his face." David had not heard this song but sang a melancholy lyric of his own misery's making. David did not hate his son Absalom. He was angered and disappointed in him. The apple of his eye had proved to be the worst apple in the barrel. Absalom had murdered his half-brother Amnon, and had fled to his wife's home in Upper Galilee to escape the long arm of the law. Yet David's deep love for Absalom would never flee his broken heart's sanctuary.

Joab was chairman of the joint chiefs of staff. Daily he watched as David's mind drifted away from strategy sessions with his generals. Daily he watched David's mind descend into the black cesspool of senility. Daily he observed the decline of the man he loved. Nor were Joab's watchful eyes closed to the people of Israel, who were losing confidence in their king and government. The great lion of the tribe of Judah had become as meek as the newborn lamb he once pressed to his bosom in a Bethlehem sheepfold.

Joab decided to revive the spirits of his commander in chief. He traveled to Tekoa, which would later cradle the head of the prophet Amos. There, on the outskirts of the barren Judean desert, he met a wise woman noted for her storytelling ability. Together Joab and the old crone created a fictitious parable. The woman dressed in black as if she were mourning. Joab saw to it that she was allowed to pass through the checkpoints guarding the entrance to the palace of Zion, usually as impregnable as an entrance to the Fort Knox mint. She was brought to David's throne, and the weary king bent his ear to her sad tale. The peasant mother told him that one day her two sons had engaged in a terrible quarrel in the fields. With tears browning her weathered face, the grieving mother implored David to forgive her first-born. She feared that, without benefit of the king's pardon, the Bedouin code of honor would demand the lad's life. Without her son she would be deprived of grandchildren; deprived of family and deprived of hope, which was the only candle beaming light into her heart's humble hovel.

David was roused from his apathy and vowed that the murderer would live. Quickly his mind saw through the tale. It was too pat. Too easily did the spurious parable mirror his own situation. For did he not also mourn a murdered son Amnon? And did he not also have a son who had murdered in cold blood? A son named Absalom who had been in exile for years. A son he longed to see from the time the sun climbed to the peaks of the Judean hills at dawn to the time his weary head was laid upon the palace pillow at night.

The exile was ended. Absalom returned to his father's kingdom. A father's love was stronger than a king's justice. Absalom would live. David had himself been guilty of murder. He had with malice aforethought plotted the death of Uriah the Hittite to win Bathsheba as his most prized paramour. David the murderer forgave Absalom who also lived by the sword.

The great American author Thomas Wolfe titled one of his novels *You Can't Go Home Again,* but you can. David welcomed home his prodigal son Absalom. Later the Son of David would tell of another father. A father who kills the fatted calf and opens his arms wide to rejoice at the return of his prodigal son.

Jesus told his parable to teach us that God is our Father. His are the everlasting arms. His door is always open, and the light of eternal life is on in the hallways of hell, when we are certain God has misplaced our zip code. The arms of Christ were stretched out upon the cross to embrace everyone. Each of us is a child of a loving father. A father who rules the universe with justice but also with love.

In all the entrances and exits we make upon the stages of life he is there. In all the problems and joys we encounter as we go through life's struggles, we can rejoice in the good news that this is our Father's world. Today he calls us to come home from exile. Today he calls us his beloved children. " 'Tis so sweet to trust in Jesus" because he is our Father who loves us as if there were no one else to love in all the universe. Hallelujah!

Labor Pains   *2 Samuel 18:1-33*

Proper 14, 15 (August 7-13, 14-20)

There was no Labor Day holiday for Tom Sutpen. Every day he had to wrestle the red-eyed Virginia sun as he bent before the plow. Each sunset he shambled off to his shack. Each night was a black abyss as he heard his children cry out for food and his wife dream of shoes for each of the little ones.

Thomas Jr. saw the seasons turn his father's hair wintry white. He smelled the whiff of death on his father's breath, and decided to follow his dream far from the blistering gaze of the Virginia delta's sun.

His journey through life was a quest for an unholy grail of pelf, paramours, and power. He became Colonel Sutpen of Mississippi. Vast plantations of white cotton stretched before the verandah where this blackhearted dictator ruled his slaves and his family with a rod of iron.

The story of Thomas Sutpen is told with brilliance by William Faulkner in his 1936 novel, *Absalom, Absalom.* Faulkner tells how Tom's two sons Henry and Charles grew to hate one another. At last, Henry's cup of wrath reached the boiling point, as it poured out in the hot blood of his murdered brother Charles. Faulkner drew many parallels in his sordid tale with the tragic story of rebellion Absalom waged against his father David.

The tale of Absalom, up in arms against his father, is one of the darkest portraits of evil displayed in the gallery of biblical baddies. Think of the fathers who are betrayed and opposed by their sons. Adam, brokenhearted at the news that Cain had cut down Abel and fled east of Eden. Gideon, learning that his son Abimelech had killed his brothers and, when trapped by the law, had killed himself. David, plucking the

broken chords of his heart's deepest grief at the way Absalom had manuevered himself into a position of power. A position allowing him to usurp, for a time, the crown of David.
Absalom loved power more than he loved his own father.

Rallying young men eager for battle and for shekels, Absalom forced David to flee with a few hundred faithful followers over the Mount of Olives. Absalom was given bad
advice. He made several military mistakes. In the forests of
Ephraim, his army was obliterated by David's guerilla-trained
warriors. Separated from his troops, he was caught in the low-
hanging branches of a terebinth oak tree. Josephus, the Jewish historian, adds that he probably hung there by his hair.
Here he was slaughtered by David's troops. Here his dreams
of glory and gold ended, as he became an intruder in the dust
of death.

Today, in Jerusalem's Kidron Valley, tour guides point out
the pillar of Absalom. Absalom, again according to Josephus,
built the pillar as a great tomb, symbolizing his greatness.
Like the Tower of Babel, it seems to represent man worshiping glory. Absalom worshiping his favorite god — the divinity
that he looked at in the mirror each morning while shaving:
himself.

Absalom was not buried in the ornate tomb Jerusalem
erected to his glorification. He lies buried in an obscure grave
— a pit where his enemies threw his corpse and covered it
with rocks.

We are not concerned about casting either stones or
aspersions at Absalom. Nor can we grieve over his death as
did David who cried in one of the greatest laments recorded,
"O my son, Absalom, my son, Absalom! Would I had died instead of you, O Absalom my son, my son!"

It was good for Israel that David regained his crown. For
with all of his faults David did try to rule his kingdom with
justice. For all of his sins David did trust in God, and not himself, as the helmsman of the ship of state.

Absalom incarnates the spirit of a bullying, bragging, and reckless agitator working like a cancerous growth in the body politic. Our age has not been immune to Absalom-minded politicians and preachers. The word "demagogue" comes from the Greek. "Demos" meaning "people" and "ago" meaning a "leader." In our parlance, though, a "demagogue" is more than a leader of the people. He is an agitator fanning the flames of mob rule. We have looked at the face of Absalom on television and heard his milk-shake smooth voice on the radio. Our age of anxiety has heard men of his ilk. The Hitlers, Mussolinis, Stalins, and Tojos no longer reign. But the Khomenis, Khadafis, and cut-throats in the little republics of Central America still seek to convince their people that everything is all right at the O.K. Corral.

In our own land it behooves us all to be on the lookout for easy answers dished up by demagoguery. We all need to be vigilant and on guard lest we fall prey to our prejudices against another race or religion in our own society. We also need to be alert to fallacious arguments convincing us of easy solutions to thorny problems supplied by hail-fellow-well-met prophets of peace, prosperity, and progress.

In 1681 poet John Dryden wrote a long satirical poem called "Absalom and Achitophel." Dryden wrote his poem shortly after the rebellious and headstrong Duke of Monmouth had fomented a plot against his father, King Charles II. Dryden, like Faulkner, saw many parallels with the tale of Absalom as told in the Bible. One theme Dryden insists upon is that a people and a democracy must demand the best from their leaders. Whenever we coddle a king or worship a preacher, prophet, or politician, we are in grave danger of bowing before false idols. Dryden put it well when he observed:

With secret joy indulgent
David viewed
His youthful image in his son renewed

To all his wishes nothing he denied
The Jews, a headstrong, moody
murmuring race . . .
God's pampered people whom
. . . no king could govern nor no
God could please.

In this rich land of pampered people, where the gods of commercialism and materialism met in joyous conclave, we are called to worship him who is the Lord of all. Christ alone who is the leader to whom we this day pledge our ultimate allegiance in the covenant of love. He as the resurrected son of David whose rebellion is against the black trinity of death, disease, and despair. His name is Jesus Christ. This day I declare before you all that, as for me and my family, we will serve the Lord God Almighty who made heaven and earth.

Faces of the Nation   *2 Samuel 19:8-15*

You see their smiling faces everywhere. They have their
own birth certificates. Their birthdays are cause for celebration. Legend has it that they are orphans who have been
found in a cabbage patch. Each toddler who clutches one of
the Cabbage Patch dolls in her arms feels as if she were a
mommy.

Cabbage Patch dolls sell out quickly and, in some cities,
near riots have occurred in stores where they have become
available. Cabbage Patch dolls became as popular as an air-
conditioner salesman in the Mohave desert. Their faces are
irresistible. So too are the furry faces of puppies and kittens,
as their eyes seem to plead with you to carry them out of the
pet store.

Faces are essential in life. It would be impossible to im-
agine a world in which everyone went headless, a la the headless horseman, terrifying an Ichabod Crane one dark and
windy colonial Halloween. Israel was a headless horseman.
She had no captain to guide her ship of state through the stormy seas. Like sheep gone astray, she bleated a fearful cry.
Vainly she looked for a shepherd to guide her through the dark
valleys of death into the sun-speckled highlands of hope.

Absalom's pied piper's promise of gold had led the nation to the black abyss of death. She had said "yes" to Absalom's gold and "no" to David's God. In the agony of defeat
she longed for the thrill of victory.

David and his merry men were flush with victory as they
encamped east of the Jordan near Gilgal, where the people
of Israel had first entered the Promised Land. David's heart
was broken over the death of Absalom. It took the blunt-
speaking commander of his armies, Joab, to remind David

that his personal grief must not impede his public triumph. David was called upon to speak to his victorious troops; he looked into the faces of these battle-bruised veterans.

Shakespeare's Henry V said to his troops before battle:

We few, we happy few, we band of brothers:
For he today that sheds his blood with me
shall be my brother.

(Henry V. *IV, iii, 60*)

It is good to gaze at the faces of those friends who are with us through thick and thin. As David gazed at the faces of his men, may we look back at those people who have stood by us in good times and in bad. So often we take for granted the love and support handed to us. We forget that, when the chips are down and we are going down for the count of ten, we are not alone. We have our family; we have our church, and we have a friend named Jesus who shall never leave our side.

Soon leaders from the quarreling tribes decided to form a delegation and come to David at Gilgal. They had learned that the price of forgiveness was cheaper by the dozen. They had patched up their hates and jealousies in their need to sew a seamless robe of reunion. Solemnly, they bowed in a salaam before the sheik of souls at Gilgal. Fervently, they called to their shepherd to once again guide his faithful flock into the future.

David responded to their pleas for help. He could never welcome his prodigal son Absalom home again. But he could embrace a prodigal people to his shepherd's breast and love and serve them. The Arabs have a proverb which says that "pardon is the choicest flower of victory."[1]

As David embraced his nation in love, we as Christians think of the Son of David. We remember how we exiled him to a cross. We remember how he crossed the Rubicon of our rejection. We recall the old spiritual line, "He's got the whole world in his hands." We reach out our hands to him and he

---

[1] *Penguin Dictionary of Proverbs*, Harmondsworth, England, 1983, p. 95.

touches us with gentle forgiveness. The faces of his army and the faces of Israel looked to the face of David for guidance. He who was the father of his country now had won the allegiance of the people to his banner. All now had been reunited in the flock of David. All had learned that a house divided against itself cannot stand. All, that is, except for a few reluctant and shame-etched faces in Judah. Judah, the tribe of which David was a lion. Judah, which had been the most zealous in the rebellious cause of Absalom. Many feared that David would exact a stern retribution on them. Their fears were allayed. David sent word to the elders of Judah, "Why should you be the last to bring the king back to his house . . .?" Judah was to be forgiven. Her war against David was to be forgotten. The sword of the lion of the tribe of Judah was broken in his broken heart. It was with shalom, and not with a sword, that David welcomed Judah back.

We face each day surrounded by faces. The army of faces who comfort us when we retreat to lick our wounds. The faces who give us the courage to face today and tomorrow. The faces of those we need to forgive, and of whom we need to be forgiven by.

God looks at millions of faces. He sees the face of the grandfathers and the faces of the infants. He sees a world of faces crying out in hunger and pain. He looks at these faces with the pain-plagued face of a carpenter from Nazareth. A carpenter who cries, "Father, forgive them for they know not what they do." A good shepherd who leads us back into the flock with care, and helps us face the music of our betrayals. A face which is eternal and everlasting. Today in our pride and folly and straying we look to him for succor. Our hope is in the face of him who is Son of God and Son of David — even Jesus the living Christ.

94

A Senior Servant   *2 Samuel 19:19-31*

Freshman servants are as easy to find as the circus-escaping elephant hiding behind a fire hydrant. Scores of fraternities and sororities are transformed into animal houses on every September day. Freshmen are turned into obedient coolies as they bow and scrape before upper classmen. Like a faithful Fido, the freshmen must minister to every need of their senior masters. It is part of the initiation process whose goal is to turn beanie-wearing frosh into proud-as-punch alumni, as they return in glory to root for old Sigma Tau.

Senior servants, on the other hand, are as hard to find on a campus as a teenager when the dishes need washing.

What is true in college frat houses is not always true in life. Look around any church on any Sunday morning. Chances are the person next to you is a senior citizen. Chances are good, too, that you yourselves are senior and seasoned veterans in that grand experience called life.

Barzillai was fourscore years old. In his rich life he had gained enough gold to turn Midas' eyes green as a gourd. He owned vast acreage. His eyes could still sparkle as they scanned the rich hillside earth he could call his own. His contentment was as deep as the good earth below his sandals. His reputation was as high as the stately trees standing silent sentinel in that gentle land east of Jordan, Gilead.

Jeremiah had asked in a moment of bereftness, "Is there a balm in Gilead?" "Yes," would have replied Barzillai. Resin from the balsam tree was used to make holy oil for the fastidious temple priests in Jerusalem. It was used to make a paste-like perfume which would have pleased the olfactory apparatus of a Coco Chanel. It would even come in handy on a camping trip as it was an effective antidote to snake bites. There was a balm in Gilead.[1]

[1] Michael Zahary, *Plants of the Bible*, Cambridge University Press, Cambridge, England, 1982, p. 198.

There was also a king in Gilead. His name was David. His son Absalom had forced him to flee from his home and to enter the woody wilderness of Gilead. Lady Antonia Fraser tells us in her book *Royal Charles* that the merry monarch Charles II once hid in a tree for several hours to escape being killed by his enemies.[2] David couldn't see the forest because he was lost in the trees. Hiding as a fugitive and seeking as a father to discover how he had turned his son Absalom into an enemy. Perhaps the questions of how and why the hatred Absalom felt for his father were never resolved in David's heart. David, the astute politician, had come to the brink of defeat. Alone, without much food, fuel, or finances, he sat in the wilderness while Absalom ruled his flock Israel.

There came to David a few faithful servants. Even in the wilderness of our doubts, and in the nights of our defeat, there are those who will not desert us. Barzillai came with wheat, barley, meal, and honey. Barzillai did not forget who was the true King of Israel. He did not abandon his faith in David or in his God.

Barzillai was the rich mogul who had worked his way through the eye of the needle. He had knitted a life of good deeds into a pattern of passionate caring for others. Barzillai was the Good Samaritan from Gilead. He was himself the balm of Gilead who healed the sin-sick soul of David with his devoted service. His faith in David and his faith in the God who chose David to rule was as strong as Bethlehem Steel. No wonder his name in Hebrew means "the man of iron."

Barzillai is not to be conceived of as a man of steel, leaping tall buildings in a single bound with Superman-like glee. He is simply a picture of servants we all know. Senior citizens who have remained faithful to the altars of their childhood homes. Veterans of church life, who have remained true to

[2] Antonio Fraser, *Royal Charles,* Alfred A. Knopf, New York, 1979.

the old kirk, when the old world had beckoned to them with the siren sweet lights of downtown skepticism.

The great Scotch preacher Alexander MacClaren put it well when speaking one night to a group of factory workers: ". . . blessed shall we be if the early faith is the faith that brightens the end . . . (a faith) . . . which begins to glow . . . as the shadows fall . . ."[3]

Barzillai asked no reward from David. The King's armies were supreme and the road to Jerusalem was open. David promised Barzillai that he would have an honored place at his court, feast at his table, and spend his remaining days garbed in rich silks. Barzillai refused to cross the Jordan with his monarch. He had discovered satisfaction in doing good for others and sharing with others. The reward of seeing David returning from exile, was the reward Barzillai desired. The reward of seeing his faith vindicated in this lion of the tribe of Judah.

Abraham Lincoln was asked daily to distribute federal jobs to his longtime cronies, and some who said they were his friends. One day he learned from his doctor that he had a case of smallpox. The physician warned Lincoln that it was contagious. Lincoln, the good physician binding the wounds of a Civil War-ravaged America, replied, "Good, at last I have something I can give to everyone!"[4]

There is still a balm in Gilead. It is dispensed by the Good Physician, the Son of David, and the Good Samaritan of us all. Today, our option is to be with freshmen in the school of Christ, or to reside with senior citizen disciples bearing battle scars aplenty, who reach out hands to others and at the same time touch the nail-scarred hands of him we call Savior, even Jesus the Christ.

[3] *Week-Day Addresses,* Funk & Wagnells Co., New York.
[4] *Presidential Anecdotes,* Boller, Penguin, 1981, p. 133.

Rock, Roll, and Remember
2 Samuel 22:8-20

The sky was Bible black with brooding menace. Heaven's lamplighter had snuffed out the starry candles of light. Thunder roared in a basso profundo voice of rage. The frail vessel climbed yet another Mount Everest of waves. Icicle-pointed raindrops stung the face with a wasp-like malice. Indigo night. The death of light. The storm and the fury.

He faced all of them. The storm was but a mirror of the hurricane of heartache, battering against his soul's coast. His faith was cobweb-thin; his nerves as frayed as a thread-bare coat. Gloom had enguifed glory. Darkness had swallowed light. Somewhere on that vast sea the young preacher wrestled with Jacob-intense might against the demons feasting on the leftovers from faith's last supper.

The Reverend Newman, on his journey from England to Italy, was not alone on that voyage of 1833. All of us have at times been cast adrift on a sea of chaotic doubt. It is at times such as these when we learn to sink or swim. Times when we are called upon to whistle in the dark. Times when the valley of the shadow of death encroaches on our turf. Times when our light brigade of festive hope seems to be ambushed by fear. Times when we need to know we are not companionless on the journey.

David knew how darkness can conquer light. In his life he had often suffered a total eclipse of the heart. He had walked through the valley of sin. With Hank Williams he could lament, "I wandered in darkness, life filled with sin, I wouldn't let my dear Savior in." With those caught in the vicious vale of gloating death, he could say with the grief-torn living, "O Absalom, O Absalom, my son, my son."

David also knew that light is stronger than dark. He knew the lamplighter of love who brightens our way home. He knew the God of stormy fury who is also the God who leads us into paths of righteousness for his name's sake. The God who spoke to Moses at Sinai and Elijah in the wilderness. The God who comforted Joseph in exile. The God who is our Good Shepherd leading us into the presence of our enemies; restoring our souls leading us into the paths of righteousness for his name's sake.

The trouble is that it is sometimes hard to hear God in a noisy age of transition. David lived in an age of change. The ancient tribal way of doing business guided by warring sheiks had been replaced by a united nation under the guidance of a king. Change was threatening to David and his people. Change also threatens and disturbs us. Alvin Toffler writes of *Future Shock. Time* scribes devote an entire issue to the "Computer Revolution." Students tell us that today an Apple a day for the teacher is a computer system, and not a luscious Washington State Golden Delicious.

David wrote his psalm in a time of new creation. He sang it in the birth throes of a new era in the life of Israel. Even as Bob Dylan, a troubadour of our own generation, has chanted, "The times, they are a changing." David went through more changes in his life than a baby experiences in the war against his Pampers super-absorbents. He had emerged from rural obscurity to rich and opulent wealth. He knew the heartbreak of grief and the flooding joy of love. He had ascended the highway to heaven and had plummeted to the abysmal depths of hell. He had known the quicksand terror of doubt, and had walked on the firm terra firma of hope.

David was not alone on his journey. He knew the companion who is ever with us. A God who is with us on the sunshiny verandah of victory. A god who is with us when the earth rocks and rolls with thunderous anger against us. A God who gives us courage to face the enemies called "doubt" and "distrust."

For when the earth and our lives are rocking and rolling with hurt, it behooves us to remember who we are and whose we are. We are children of God. We are sons and daughters of the universe. We are brothers and sisters united in love. We are disciples of the Son of David and are called to be his ambassadors of love.

Christ will reach down from on high and take us in his arms. He is the bridge over troubled waters. He it is who will deliver us from our demons, because he delights in we who are his children.

So when the foundations shake and the earth rumbles with trouble, let us remember that God is in charge and will not desert us. Paul Tillich, the great German theologian, said, "When the earth grows old and wears out, when nations and cultures die, the Eternal changes the garments of his infinite being. He is the foundation on which all foundations are laid; and this foundation cannot be changed," (*The Shaking of the Foundations,* Scribner's and Sons, New York, 1948, p. 9).

John Henry Newman, the young pastor we met earlier in this chapter, did not remain alone between the stormy sky and the raging waves. His soul was quieted and his faith in God gave him a buoy to guide him home. He went below to his cabin and wrote, "Lead, kindly Light, amid the encircling gloom. Lead Thou me on! The night is dark and I am far from home; Lead Thou me on!"

May God lead each of us through the weeks ahead. May we all be guided by the stong beams of hope emanating from that lighthouse of love called the church. May the Son of David, even Jesus the Christ be our pilot into the future.

Love's Legacy

Swan Song of a shepherd. Climactic cadenza to a pastoral symphony written by a Bethlehem bard. The lion of the tribe of Judah in the winter of his days. A lion roaring out a legacy of love to the ages. A grizzled veteran of life's battles facing the specter of death with the courage expressed so well by Dylan Thomas:

Do not go gentle into that good night
Old age should burn and rave at close of day;
Rage, Rage, against the dying of the light.

David roared against injustice in his last will and testament. He remembered God's faithful love for him in all his trials and travails. He looked forward to a day when a new king would come who would shine his love throughout the earth.

The world has always delighted in recording the last words of famous people. O'Henry died saying, "Turn up the lights, I don't want to go home in the dark." Ballerina Anna Pavlova died crying out, "Get my swan costume ready." Legend has it that an expiring Oscar Wilde complained, "Either that wallpaper goes, or I do." Rock musician Terry Kath, playing Russian roulette with a loaded pistol, remarked, "Don't worry, it isn't loaded." My grandmother told me that, in her day, when folks usually died at home, the family often gathered around the deathbed to hear a loved one's final words.

Today you may remember the last words spoken to you by someone you loved. In this chapter we hear the last words of one of our great fathers of faith. David's strong booming voice rings down the ages as he rang down the curtain on one of the greatest lives ever lived. Joseph Heller in his satirical new novel about David, begins his fiction with David saying, "I have the best story in the Bible."

Perhaps he does. For in a pre-Christian age, David was a Renaissance man. He was a warrior, a poet, an outstanding administrator and ruler. He was a great sinner and an even greater saint. He knew profound despair and great joy.

Julius Caesar gave the citizens of Rome money, causing them to rejoice in the crowded streets of the eternal city as the dictator's will was read. Billionaire Howard Hughes' will has been disputed for years as various people wrangle for the wampum. Several rich eccentrics appear in the press after leaving their fortunes to dogs, cats, or other pets. David left us nothing that we can touch, taste, or try on. He did, however, leave us a will that reminds each of us that we are living in the will of God.

David came from a desert tribe acquainted with the parched feel of dry earth. He knew the suffering of those enduring long summer droughts and famine. He knew, too, the joy of gentle rain upon the fields. He tells us that a good ruler is like the rain which makes grass sprout from the earth. An earth cluttered with weeds and thistles yielding to flowers. Flowers garbed in technicolored pastels dancing a light fantastic across fields of emerald green. David says that a just ruler is like this rain. A wise and good leader is like sunshine on a cloudless morning. In his final will he prayed that his people would be governed by good rulers. His hope was not realized in Israel. But reading the will, we do know that "in the dark streets shineth the everlasting light." Out of Bethlehem winter bleakness would emerge a ruler, a good shepherd whose name is Jesus.

David reminded us in his will that he was anointed as God's servant. He remembered that he anointed his head with oil and his cup runneth over. Perhaps as we read these words we can remind ourselves that in the waters of Baptism we have been anointed as God's children. Perhaps we can pledge ourselves to serving the God of David with obedient love.

Perhaps too we can worship him who was anointed in the Jordan by John the Baptizer. Him who makes us lie down in green pastures, restoreth our souls and leads us in the paths of righteousness for his name's sake. Him whom we call the Christ of Creation, even Jesus the Christ.

David speaks from his deathbed to make us aware that we are partners in an everlasting covenant with God. God's covenant has been sealed with the blood of the Lamb slain for our sins. It is renewed each time we break the bread and sip the cup of the New Testament in the Sacrament of Communion.

David says that he has been a sweet singer of psalms. How many millions of people have been the beneficiaries of his spiritual legacy to the race of humanity as recorded in the Psalms? How many souls have been comforted in grief by the Twenty-third Psalm? How many hearts have been healed by his immortal songs of hope? The Psalms stand as one of the great utterances of our humanity.

The sweet singer of psalms is the kingly forbear of him who sings salvation's song from a cross of shame. Him whose name is the Christ who sings Easter hymns on that great resurrection morn, when he muted death's dirge in the great crescendo of resurrected life hymned to the heavens.

David's last will and testament gives each of us hope as we recall past blessings, present mercies, and look forward to a future hope of glory as we await the coming of Christ the Son of David, the Son of God.

Strong Words

1 Kings 2:1-4, 10-12

Proper 17 (August 28-September 3)

Words are like men and women. Some are as weak as a scarecrow's handshake. Other words are as strong as Mr. Skunk's fragrant odor after he munches down a bermuda onion. Words are important.

David knew the importance of words. The words of his poetry will shine in the firmament of faith's blue skies forever. David's joys and sorrows, mountain tops and valleys were best expressed in words.

David also knew fathers were important. He who had been raised by a simple father in a burg called Bethlehem. He who had watched his father's flocks and kept them from the ravening wolf and the wily rustler. He who had raised ten sons and seen them fight and claw for his tottering throne. His children had disappointed him and exalted him.

The psalmist sings his swan song in our passage. He gives to Solomon strong words before the curtain closes on the stage.

> It is almost night again. The skies of the desert are turning brown. In the pools of lamplight smoldering in the shadows I see an eager bright-eyed youth ... he is holding a lyre with eight strings ... He is ruddy ... His neck is as a tower of ivory ... His locks are bushy, and black as a raven ... his head is as ... fine gold ... His music is soothing, almost divine. [1]

David is looking into the eyes of his son Solomon. He is a father whispering goodbye to his son, his nation, and his home.

We have a father who loves us when we lose and when we loaf. A father whose footstep catches our ears as we flee

[1] Joseph Heller, *God Knows*, Alfred A. Knopf, New York, New York, 1984, pp. 352-353.

him down the years. A father who picks us up and carries us to his home. May we as parents and children learn to love each other. May we be open to each other's cries of pains and shouts of joy.

"Sunrise, sunset," sings Tevia in "Fiddler on the Roof." The years swiftly pass and we cannot halt their blitzkrieg through time. We can pause and refresh one another with the gift of open, giving love.

A cannibal chief roasted a missionary for lunch, and by so doing acquired a taste for religion. In our day when the family is attacked, the role of the church and family togetherness are vital. Some say that if absence makes the heart grow fonder, a lot of people must love the church.

A father does not send his children to church. A good father does not force them to go to church. A good father does show them through example that the worship of our heavenly father is important. What we do often outshouts what we say.

Ken Chafin, a professor at the Southern Baptist Seminary in Louisville, Kentucky, has written a book entitled *Is There a Family in the House?* One night he had to lecture to an audience about fatherhood. Chafin asked his daughter to suggest a few qualties she thought went into making a father. She said a good father can:

1. catch a fish
2. build a fire
3. fly a kite
4. catch a butterfly
5. plant a flower
6. get a kitty-cat out of the mud.[2]

Fathers are leaders. Unlike David, they are most often men doing their best for their families, their employers, and God.

[2] Ken Chafin, *Is There a Family in the House?,* World Wide Publications, Minneapolis, n.d., p. 98.

We too have a Father — a Father of one who prayed to him in the stark wilderness of Judea and in the lush mountain crags of Galilee, one who followed him upon the high road of service and cried in anguish to him in the black night of Gethsemane.

In the beginning was the Word — at the end is a waiting Father eager to greet his prodigal children.